target to table

healthy and delicious meals one superfood at a time

by kristen johnson and matt johnson

target to table

healthy and delicious meals
one superfood at a time

by kristen johnson and matt johnson

Photographs by Matthew Wesener
Design by Design 2

ontarget
LIVING

Printed in Malaysia

10 9 8 7 6 5 4 3 2 1

ISBN 978-0-9727281-7-1

ontargetliving.com

Photography: Matthew Wesener
Design: Design 2
Editor: Paula Johnson
Copy editor: Bonney Mayers
Cover photography: True Productions

DISCLAIMER
This publication contains the opinions and ideas of its authors. Neither the
publisher nor the authors are responsible for your specific health or allergy
needs that may require medical supervision, or for any adverse reactions to the
recipes contained in this book. It is sold with the understanding that the authors
and publisher are not engaged in rendering medical, health, or any other kind
of personal professional services in the book. The reader should consult his or
her medical, health or other competent professional before adopting any of the
suggestions in this book or drawing inferences from it. The authors and publisher
specifically disclaim all responsibility for any liability, loss, or risk, personal or
otherwise, which is incurred as a consequence, directly or indirectly, or the use
and application of the contents of this book.

We want to thank our amazing mother Paula for teaching us how to make food that combines love and flavor, and especially for all of your editorial, organizational, and secretarial expertise, and long, hard hours putting this book together.

Thank you to our father Chris for your inspiration, love, and for always encouraging us to find our passion.

You both totally rock and we feel so lucky to call you ours.

contents

foreword

We at On Target Living are very proud and excited to bring our **Target to Table** cookbook to you! What makes *Target to Table* unique is the quality and taste of each recipe. The recipes are simple, fun to make, extremely healthy, and taste and look fantastic. We wanted to create a cookbook that not only had wonderful recipes to choose from, but also helped educate you the reader along the way—encouraging you to adopt the On Target Living Lifestyle! This is our second cookbook and was conceived around our On Target Living Principles.

The relationship we have with food impacts our lives in so many ways. What we eat, how we eat, when we eat, and why we eat all play a significant role in our health, our energy, our emotions, and our vitality. Food is a big deal to most people!

Many people have beliefs around food that may hinder health, performance, and happiness. Some believe that healthy food tastes bad, carbohydrates make you fat, all calories are created equal, eating healthy costs too much, or healthy cooking requires lots of time. If even one of these statements rings true to you, we hope to dispel those limiting beliefs through recipes that are delicious, satisfying, affordable, and easy to make.

I learned at a young age the power of food and the tremendous impact it can have on your life! I developed major skin problems which started around the age of 8 and continued into my early 20's. I was prescribed oral medications and topical creams, but nothing seemed to work. The doctors told my parents, "Your son just has sensitive skin." I did not have sensitive skin—it was my poor diet wreaking havoc with my skin. As I started learning more about nutrition and improved my diet, my skin problems slowly disappeared.

Do you remember the song in the classic movie *Mary Poppins* that included the words medicine and sugar? Mary Poppins would sing over and over, "Just a spoon full of sugar helps the medicine go down." Hippocrates once said, "Let Food Be Your Medicine and Medicine Be Your Food." Food is a powerful medicine, and when chosen and prepared correctly, there's no need for the sugar!

In 2006, after working in the health and fitness industry for over twenty years and logging more than 17,000 hours of one-on-one coaching, I decided to take my message out on the road and founded On Target Living. I began traveling the country speaking to corporations, associations, and schools, sharing the On Target Living Lifestyle—REST EAT MOVE.

I learned a long time ago that the greatest results are found by working toward a balanced lifestyle that includes getting enough rest, fueling your body with high quality foods and beverages, and moving your body on a daily basis. Nothing fancy—just sustainable lifestyle habits that can be enjoyable, repeatable, and most importantly—create amazing results!

The On Target Living brand is based off the Food Target. I developed the Food Target in 1994 to help people learn how to easily upgrade their food choices, focusing on food quality not just calories! The Food Target focuses on a balance of carbohydrates, proteins, and fats while incorporating an assessment of the quality of their nutrients. The lowest nutritional value foods are located on the outside red area of the Food Target. The highest quality foods, foods in their most natural state including many superfoods, are closer to the green center of the Target.

Superfoods are nutritionally dense foods that keep the body healthy and help you perform at your best. Today my nutritional plan includes many superfoods, such as wheatgrass, spirulina/chlorella, cod liver oil, flaxseeds, cacao nibs, coconut, pumpkin seeds, hemp seeds, macadamia nuts, Brazil nuts, almonds, white figs, dried mango, oatmeal, greens, sweet potatoes, broccoli, dark cherries, raspberries, lemons, and limes.

Our mission at On Target Living is to help people live a healthy and happy life by adopting a healthy lifestyle. Our mantra is "Small Steps to Healthy Living!"

Our number one goal in *Target to Table* is to share our passion and love for food with you and others who want to have food that is truly healthy, energizing, simple, easy, fun, and most importantly, tastes fantastic!

I would like to end by thanking my kids Kristen and Matt, my wife Paula, Bonney our editor, Cindy our designer, and Matt our photographer. All did a wonderful job putting this cookbook together. It really was a team effort.

Wishing you a lifetime of Health & Happiness—Bon Appétit!

Chris Johnson
Founder and CEO
On Target Living

introduction

Born one minute apart, we were no ordinary siblings. Our upbringing was no less unusual. Under our father's influence we were weaned on flaxseeds, cod liver oil, and other freakishly healthy foods. Yuck, right? We didn't know any better.

Our mother, however, taught us how to cook. By the time we were eight years old, we were preparing family dinners once a week and "busting suds" on our nights off. Our family bond was forged celebrating tasty creations and fighting over failures.

It was during childhood that our father Chris Johnson created the Food Target that we know and love. Visually, the concept was and remains simple. The closer the ring is to the center, the healthier the foods. At the very center are the healthiest foods - the superfoods. We came to understand the Target was much more than a colorful circle. See Food Target page xii.

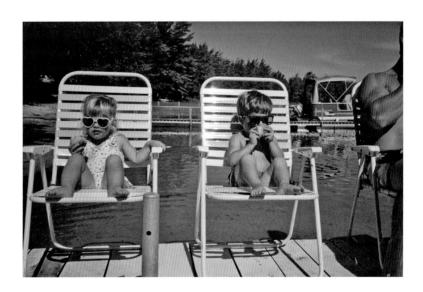

As we grew older, with a refrigerator stocked full of superfoods, we learned how to make food actually taste good and created meals that were healthy and delicious. We started weeding out the less nutritious ingredients from our family's famed recipes and adding *one superfood at a time.*

Why butter? Why not virgin coconut oil?

Why processed sugar? Raw organic honey is plenty sweet.

Why chocolate chips? How about cacao nibs?

The Food Target was working its magic. We were taking "Small Steps to Healthy Living." We like to think that many recipes were improved and others inspired from this undertaking.

In *Target to Table*, we teamed up to share our culinary repertoire with you. Not all of these recipes call for true superfoods, but they will get you started on your quest to move towards the center of the Food Target. Who says healthy cooking can't be fun, delicious and easy all at the same time. Heck, we have a 3-ingredient recipe for banana ice cream!

Creating healthy and delicious meals one superfood at a time means taking those small steps at the store and in the kitchen to develop healthy, lifelong eating habits for you and your family.

From Target to Table, we hope you enjoy these recipes as much as we do!

Kristen & Matt Johnson

food target

BY CHRIS JOHNSON

a guide to getting the target to your table

This section includes principles to get you from the shopping cart to the plate. We have provided a basic 101 education on nutrition, digestion, how to read a food label, when to buy organic, what cooking oils to use, and more.

We have chosen not to include the nutritional breakdown for our recipes. That's because the closer you eat to the center of the Food Target the less likely you are to overeat, and therefore you don't have to worry about counting calories, or anything else for that matter. Since the center green circle foods are closer to the "Source", they keep you feeling more nourished and satisfied.

superfoods 101

Superfoods are nutrient-rich foods, such as fruits, vegetables, ancient grains, healthy fats, and lean proteins, considered to be especially beneficial for health and well-being. The focus of this cookbook is to help you learn how to gradually replace not-so-healthy ingredients with more nutritious items such as the superfoods found in the center green circles of the Food Target. See Food Target at left.

the source 101

Source (sôrs, sōrs)
n.
1. The point at which something springs into being or from which it derives or is obtained.
    American Heritage Dictionary

On Target Living bases its teachings on three principles: the Source, Cellular Health, and pH Balance*.

The first of these principles is the Source. Almost every food we eat today is derived from one of the three oldest foods on the planet: grass, algae, and sea vegetables. No one wants to base a diet exclusively on these three foods. However, if you focus on eating foods that are as close to their natural source as possible, you will be practicing the Source principle. So if you are looking for the most nutritious, inexpensive, less processed foods, then the closer you are to the Source the better.

The diagram on page 2 illustrates the progression of food from its original source to a more processed source.

* For more information about On Target Living, visit *ontargetliving.com*.

THE REAL THING		MORE PROCESSED*
APPLE	APPLESAUCE	APPLE JUICE
TOMATO	SALSA	KETCHUP
OAT GROATS	ROLLED OATS	INSTANT OATMEAL
FLAXSEEDS	FLAXSEED OIL	FLAXSEED OIL CAPSULES
SPROUTED BREAD	WHOLE WHEAT BREAD	WHITE BREAD
SWEET POTATOES	WHITE POTATOES	FAST FOOD FRIES
ORGANIC CHICKEN	CHICKEN	CHICKEN NUGGETS
WILD-CAUGHT FISH	FARM-RAISED FISH	FISHSTICKS

When buying more processed foods like breadcrumbs, cereals, chips, crackers, condiments, broths, soups, etc., choose an organic variety if available.

nutrition 101*

Nutrition is the process of absorbing nutrients from food and processing them in the body in order to keep you healthy and nourished. When you eat or drink, the body breaks down the nutrients and uses them for fuel, growth, and repair. Even with all of the food we currently consume in the United States, it still may be possible to be deficient in valuable nutrients.

There are two types of nutritional deficiencies:

• A primary nutrient deficiency occurs when the body lacks a specific nutrient, such as vitamin C, iodine, zinc, magnesium, or omega-3 fats.

• A secondary deficiency occurs when the body fails to absorb or utilize the foods or beverages consumed. Eating closer to the Source will ensure the nutrient absorption of these higher quality foods.

The closer you eat to the Source, the less likely you will be to have a nutrient deficiency.

*See *On Target Living: A Guide to a Life of Balance, Energy, & Vitality* for more information.

digestion 101

Ninety percent of our immune system is based on our digestive health. We have seen an explosion in the amount of digestive health problems, from acid reflux to irritable bowel, constipation, diarrhea, gluten intolerance, food allergies, bloating and gas, skin problems, asthma, cancer, headaches, low energy, inflammation, and type-2 diabetes. The digestive aids aisle in most grocery stores and pharmacies continues to expand.

Having a balanced pH in the digestive tract is crucial for optimal digestion and absorption. The stomach needs to be acidic, the small intestine more alkaline, and the large intestine a neutral pH. Balancing pH may take some time if you are currently consuming too many processed, acidic foods and beverages. If your body is too acidic, you will leach out vital minerals including calcium, magnesium, and iodine. Consuming more alkaline-based foods and beverages is your first step in balancing your pH, along with daily exercise and controlling your stress. See pH table page 5.

Tips to Improve Digestion and Gut Health

- Avoid processed foods.
- Drink half your body weight in ounces of water every day.
- Chew your food.
- Avoid liquid diets. They do not stimulate the digestive enzymes produced from chewing and can bypass many of the gastrointestinal pathways.
- Eat more "live" foods. An apple turns brown when you bite into it because it is a live food containing enzymes.
- Include fermented foods, such as kefir, kombucha, kimchee, napa cabbage, and sauerkraut.
- Balance your pH by eating more alkaline forming foods such as fruits and vegetables. See pH table page 5.
- Control your stress with exercise, deep breathing, and sleep.
- Eat foods high in chlorophyll, such as wheatgrass, spirulina/chlorella, and leafy greens.
- Add some "friendly bacteria" to the gut by taking a daily probiotic.
- Get sunlight.
- Get up and move.

Gut Superfoods

- Ginger
- Turmeric
- Mint leaves
- Licorice root
- Organic coconut

- Organic virgin coconut oil
- Chlorella/spirulina
- Wheatgrass juice
- Raw apple cider vinegar

Gut Villains

- Non-organic meat and dairy products
- HFCS (high fructose corn syrup)
- GMOs (genetically modified organisms)
- MSG (monosodium glutamate)
- Synthetic colors
- Artificial or "natural" flavors and sweeteners
- Gluten
- Antibiotics
- Medications
- DPA (diphenylamine) – the wax coating on apples
- Chlorine found in tap water
- Potassium bromate in bread
- Stress
- Lack of exercise
- Lack of sleep

To maintain a balanced pH, shoot for 65 to 70 percent of all your food and beverage sources coming from the alkaline portion of the pH table.

pH table

		More alkaline	Least alkaline	Least acidic	More acidic	Most acidic
Condiments Spices Sweeteners	baking soda, sea salt	cinnamon, most spices, molasses	most herbs, rice syrup	curry, honey, maple syrup, stevia/agave nectar	vanilla, MSG, Splenda, organic sugar	nutmeg, table salt, pudding, jam/jelly, artificial sweeteners, sugar, cocoa
Beverages	mineral water, lemon/lime water	spring/artesian water, green tea	tap water, ginger tea, herbal tea	purified water, white tea, organic coffee, red wine	distilled water, black tea, white wine	soda pop, energy drinks, coffee, alcohol/beer
Dairy Plant-Based Milk		human breast, almond, & hazelnut milks	ghee, rice, oat, hemp, & coconut milks	butter, yogurt, goat milk, goat cheese	casein, organic cow's milk, soy milk, cottage cheese	ice cream, cow's milk, processed cheese
Meat Seafood Eggs			fish	shrimp, turkey/chicken, game meat, eggs	pork, veal, lean red meat	lobster, hot dogs, deli meat, fast-food, burgers
Grains Cereal			wild rice, quinoa, oats, farro	brown rice, amaranth, millet, kashi	wheat, white rice, rye, spelt	barley, corn
Nuts Oils	pumpkin seeds	almonds, cod liver oil, evening primrose oil, sesame seeds	flaxseed oil, extra virgin olive oil, organic virgin coconut oil, most seeds	pine nuts, safflower oil, almond	sesame oil, peanuts	pecans, brazil nuts, palm kernel oil, fried food, lard, walnuts
Beans Legumes	lentils			pinto beans, lima beans, kidney beans	navy/red beans, split peas, white beans, beans, most legumes	soybeans, tempeh, chickpeas
Vegetables	sea vegetables, broccoli, yams, barley grass, wheatgrass, asparagus, sweet potato, kale, parsley	eggplant, bell peppers, cauliflower, collard greens, garlic sprouts, cabbage, pumpkin	squash, lettuce, beets, cucumber, brussels sprouts	spinach, zucchini, string beans	peas, carrots	
Fruits	lime, pineapple, nectarine, watermelon, raspberries, tangerine	apple, kiwi, peach, blackberries, grapefruit, melon, mango, lemon, avocado	orange, banana, blueberries, strawberries	dried fruit, figs, dates, plum, coconut		

gluten-free 101

Gluten is the protein found in grains such as wheat, rye, and barley. Gluten is found in products such as breads, pizza, pasta, baked goods, cereals, and many processed foods, salad dressings, and sauces. The protein in gluten may be difficult for the body to break down if a person has digestion issues leading to gluten intolerance. Many people are truly gluten intolerant. However, the reason most people have problems breaking down gluten may be due to weak digestion.

Additionally, when you are eating foods closer to the center of the Food Target and the Source, you tend to naturally eat gluten-free. Here's a look at some foods that are naturally gluten-free.

Fruits	Buckwheat	Seeds
Vegetables	Wheatgrass	flaxseeds, chia seeds,
Quinoa	Corn	hemp seeds
Oats	Potatoes	Healthy fats
Millet	Beans	coconut, olive & fish oil
Teff	Nuts	Meat
Rice		Seafood

Question:

If you remove gluten from a product, is that closer or further from the source?

Answer:

Further...makes you wonder: is gluten really the problem?

grains 101

Grain-free may be the new craze, but for most people a grain-free diet offers few benefits. In fact, it may even bring unwanted results, such as a deficiency in B vitamins, essential minerals, and problems with brain function and sleep. This way of eating is also difficult to maintain long term.

The complex of B vitamins includes eight different vitamins. Whole grains serve as a good source of several B vitamins, including thiamin, riboflavin, niacin, and folate. Thiamin, riboflavin and niacin help your body efficiently break down carbohydrates to use for energy. Folic acid, also known as folate or vitamin B-9, supports the formation and maintenance of new cells. Getting the recommended 400 mcg of folic acid

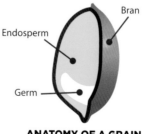

ANATOMY OF A GRAIN

per day, according to the Institute of Medicine's Food and Nutrition Board, is especially important for women of childbearing age, as a deficiency may cause birth defects during the early weeks of pregnancy.

Whole grains also contain essential vitamins such as potassium, magnesium, zinc, and iron. Potassium supports normal heart function, helping to control blood pressure. Magnesium helps to absorb calcium and relax the mind and body helping to improve sleep. Zinc is important for cell metabolism and hormonal balance, while iron is needed to produce proteins and enzymes necessary for the body.

In general, grains serve as a good source of carbohydrates, the type of macronutrient the body uses for energy and brain food. Your body needs at least 400 calories a day from grains for optimal brain function. Because the outermost portion of the grain contains the majority of the vitamins, minerals, and fiber, eating whole grains that contain the bran, germ, and endosperm intact is healthier than eating refined grains that have had the bran and germ removed.

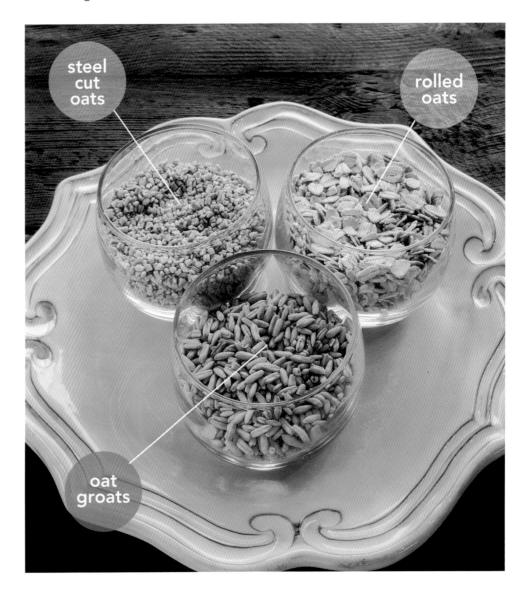

taste 101

Taste continues to be first and foremost when it comes to the way people think about food. Not far behind is nutrition and health. Most people want to eat food that is healthy, but they are not willing to sacrifice taste. As you will see from this cookbook, healthy food can taste great!

There are five types of receptors on the tongue that sense the flavors we taste: sour, sweet, salty, bitter, and umami. Each of these flavors can act on its own, but how they interact with each other is essential to making food taste delicious. Activation of any one taste will enhance another taste. Blending these tastes together is the foundation for great tasting healthy recipes.

All of these tastes can be found in the following fruits and vegetables.

Taste	Foods
Sour	Citrus fruits (lemons, limes, oranges), kiwi, blueberries
Sweet	Apples, watermelon, grapes, pears, carrots, sweet potatoes, beets
Salty	Celery, rhubarb, bok choy, sea vegetables
Bitter	Leafy greens (arugula, kale)
Umami*	Tomatoes, mushrooms, raw corn, truffle oil

Umami is a Japanese word that describes a meaty or savory taste. Tomatoes and mushrooms are high in free-form glutamate which provides a natural umami flavor. Roasting or sautéing will further intensify this flavor.

All tastes contribute to a well-balanced diet as the foods that make up each contain several essential nutrients. Usually when all five tastes are incorporated into a meal, you feel satisfied and less likely to overeat. Adding a squeeze of lemon to cooked dishes can quickly satisfy the sour taste, while adding a side of greens will fulfill the bitter taste. (See recipe for 5 Taste Salad on page 89.)

organic 101

Organic food is produced without using pesticides, herbicides, fungicides, antibiotics, and fertilizers made from synthetic ingredients. Organic meat, poultry, eggs, and dairy products come from animals that are not fed or given pesticides, growth hormones, or antibiotics.

Try to buy these products whenever possible to avoid consuming residual pesticides, antibiotics, and growth hormones.

- Organic dairy (milk, cottage cheese, cheese, yogurt)
- Organic poultry
- Wild game
- Grass-fed beef
- Wild-caught fish

When choosing to buy organic fruits and vegetables, start with the "Dirty Dozen." These are fruits and vegetables that have the highest pesticide levels. These become more important if you plan to eat the skin on these products.

Dirty Dozen (high pesticide levels)

- Apples
- Bell peppers
- Carrots
- Celery
- Cherries
- Grapes
- Lettuce
- Nectarines
- Peaches
- Pears
- Spinach
- Strawberries

Cleaner Dozen (low pesticide levels)

- Asparagus
- Avocado
- Bananas
- Broccoli
- Cauliflower
- Kiwi
- Mangos
- Onions
- Peas
- Pineapple
- Sweet potatoes
- Tomatoes

Say "No" to GMO

GMOs (genetically modified organisms) are plants or animals created through gene-splicing techniques. This technology combines DNA from different species, creating combinations of plant and animal genes that cannot be found in nature or in traditional crossbreeding. GMOs were developed to offer benefits to the consumer such as increased yield, greater protection from herbicides and drought, and enhanced nutrition. A growing body of evidence shows that the claims of many of these consumer benefits are not true, and GMOs have been connected with health problems, environmental damage, and violation, of farmers and consumers' rights.

Current GMO High-Risk Foods

- Alfalfa
- Canola
- Corn
- Soy
- Sugar beets

Common Ingredients Derived from GMO High-Risk Crops

- Amino acids, aspartame, ascorbic acid, vitamin C, citric acid
- Sodium citrate, ethanol, flavorings, high fructose corn syrup
- Hydrolyzed vegetable protein, lactic acid, maltodextrins, MSG
- Sucrose, textured vegetable protein, xanthan gum, vitamins, and yeast products

These GMO ingredients are in everything from bread, salad dressings, crackers, frozen pizza, soda pop—almost everywhere you look.

To avoid consuming GMO products, eat more organic whole foods, fewer processed foods, beverages, and supplements, and look for the non-GMO Verified Seal. That seal features brands enrolled in the Non-GMO Project, a nonprofit organization committed to providing consumers with clearly labeled Non-GMO food choices.

Notice the PLU label on the fruits and vegetables

- If it has a **5-digit code** and begins with a **9**, it means that it was organically grown.

- If the label has a **4-digit code**, it means that it was conventionally grown but not organic.

- If it has a **5-digit code** and begins with an **8**, it means that it was genetically modified. However, producers are not yet required to label GMO foods so foods with a 4-digit PLU code could contain GMOs.

cooking 101

Here are some tips to use while cooking and eating your way through the book.

- Use the Food Target as a guide for shopping and cooking. The center green circles contain the most nutritious and most flavorful foods.

- Choose extra virgin or expeller pressed oils such as extra virgin olive oil or virgin coconut oil. See Cooking Oil Guide at right.

- When using salt, choose natural sea salt. Celtic sea salt contains the most iodine.

- Use one-ingredient foods as much as possible, as they provide the most flavor and nutrition. For example: oats, quinoa, broccoli, apples

- If choosing packaged foods, avoid products that have a long ingredient list or unfamiliar ingredients.

- Choose "natural" products that are minimally processed:
    No high fructose corn syrup, refined sugars, or artificial sweeteners
    No hydrogenated oils (trans fats)
    No refined flours or milled grains
    No artificial food colorings, flavorings, or preservatives
    No GMOs

Cooking Oil Guide

This cooking oil chart includes the highest quality oils best used in cooking. Higher quality oil equals more nutrition and flavor.

For high temperature cooking, select cooking oil with a high smoke point. Heating an oil above its smoke point produces toxic fumes and harmful free radicals. Usually the more refined the oil the higher the smoke point. High quality oils tend to have lower smoke points and contain more flavor and nutrition.

Oil	Smoke Point	Uses
Pumpkin Seed Oil	320°F	Best used for no heat cooking; dressings, dips
Walnut Oil (Unrefined)	320°F	Salad dressings Add to cold dishes to enhance flavor
Organic Virgin Coconut Oil	350°F	Low to medium heat cooking, sautéing, salad oils/dressings Substitute for processed oils/butters
Red Palm Oil (Virgin, Unrefined)	350°F	Medium heat cooking, sautéing and frying, cooking/drizzling on popcorn
Extra Virgin Olive Oil	375°F	Low to medium heat cooking, sautéing, salad oils/dressings Substitute for processed vegetable oils
Macadamia Nut Oil	390°F	Low heat cooking, sautéing, salad dressings
Almond Oil	420°F	Medium-high heat cooking, sautéing, frying
Grapeseed Oil	420°F	Medium-high heat cooking, sautéing, grilling Mild flavor
Sesame Oil	450°F	High heat cooking, deep frying
Avocado Oil	520°F	High heat cooking, sautéing, frying

healthy food substitutions 101

Ingredient	Healthy Substitution
Bacon	Organic bacon, turkey bacon
Bouillon cubes	Chicken broth, vegetable broth, bone broth
Bottled dressings	Extra virgin olive oil mixed with balsamic vinegar or lemon juice
Bread/wraps for sandwiches	Lettuce wraps, collard greens , coconut wraps, sprouted grain wraps
Breadcrumbs	Shredded coconut, coconut flour, quinoa flour, almond meal, hemp seeds
Butter/oil in baking	Organic butter from grass-fed cows, organic virgin coconut oil, puréed pumpkin, mashed bananas, applesauce
Butter/oil in cooking	Organic butter from grass-fed cows, organic virgin coconut oil
Buttermilk (1 cup)	1 tablespoon lemon juice plus enough organic almond milk to make 1 cup. Let sit 5 minutes.
Canned fruit in heavy syrup	Fresh fruit or canned fruit in 100% fruit juice
Cheese	Organic cheese, goat cheese, sheep feta
Chips	Kale chips
Chocolate chips	Dark chocolate chips, cacao nibs
Coffee	Teeccino herbal coffee, organic coffee, organic green tea, herbal teas
Cornstarch/thickeners	Chia seeds, sea vegetable flakes (agar agar), potato starch
Crackers & cheese	Veggies & hummus
Cream/creamers	Organic dairy creamers, cashew milk, almond milk, coconut milk
Egg	1 tablespoon ground flaxseeds mixed with 3 tablespoons water or 1 tablespoon chia seeds with 6 tablespoons water Let sit 10 minutes. ¼ cup puréed prunes, pumpkin, squash, or applesauce
Frosting	Organic powdered sugar, Coconut Butter Frosting (see recipe page 187)

Ingredient	Healthy Substitution
Ice cream	Banana ice cream (see recipe page 188.)
Jam/Jelly	Organic pure fruit spreads; apple, cherry or grape butter
Mashed white potatoes	Mashed sweet potatoes, cauliflower, or root vegetables
Mayonnaise	Mashed avocado or organic nonfat Greek yogurt mixed with 1 teaspoon organic sugar, 1 teaspoon apple cider vinegar, salt & black pepper
Microwave popcorn	Popcorn prepared in virgin coconut oil (see recipe page 51)
Milk	Almond milk, cashew milk, -coconut milk, oat milk, hemp milk
Peanut butter	Natural peanut butter, cashew butter, almond butter
Pectin (in jam)	Chia gel (chia seeds mixed with water in a 1:6 ratio)
Salt	Herbs & spices, garlic & onion powder, ground dried mushrooms, kelp, Celtic sea salt
Sour cream	Organic nonfat plain Greek yogurt
Soy Sauce	Bragg's Liquid Aminos, coconut aminos
Sugar	Homemade applesauce (see recipe page 54.), puréed dried fruit like dates and figs, honey, agave nectar, maple syrup, molasses, stevia, vanilla extract
Sugary beverages/cocktails	Water with fresh fruit, such as sliced lemons, limes or oranges. (see mineral water cocktail recipe page 20.)
Traditional pie crust	Raw fruit and nut crust (see recipe page 192), Oatmeal Crust (see recipe page 44)
White bread	Whole wheat, whole grain, sprouted bread/wraps
White flour	White whole wheat flour, almond flour, coconut flour
White pasta	Whole grain pasta, spaghetti squash, black bean pasta, lentil pasta, mung bean pasta, spiral cut zucchini
White rice	Wild or long-grain rice, quinoa

smoothie 101

Use this as a guide to build your perfect smoothie. Simply start with a liquid, toss in fruit, throw in greens, build in protein, and add healthy fats. Bump up the nutrition even more by adding "Superpower Smoothie Superfoods" from the list at right.

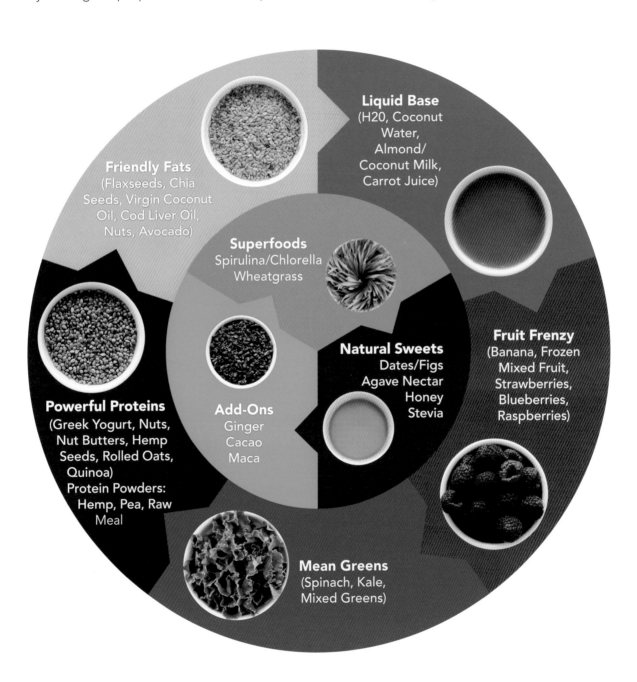

Liquid Base
(H20, Coconut Water, Almond/ Coconut Milk, Carrot Juice)

Friendly Fats
(Flaxseeds, Chia Seeds, Virgin Coconut Oil, Cod Liver Oil, Nuts, Avocado)

Superfoods
Spirulina/Chlorella Wheatgrass

Fruit Frenzy
(Banana, Frozen Mixed Fruit, Strawberries, Blueberries, Raspberries)

Natural Sweets
Dates/Figs Agave Nectar Honey Stevia

Powerful Proteins
(Greek Yogurt, Nuts, Nut Butters, Hemp Seeds, Rolled Oats, Quinoa)
Protein Powders: Hemp, Pea, Raw Meal

Add-Ons
Ginger Cacao Maca

Mean Greens
(Spinach, Kale, Mixed Greens)

Superpower Smoothie Superfoods

Cacao

Cacao is the raw unprocessed form of chocolate and is high in magnesium, manganese, zinc, and iron. Cacao has many benefits including brain health, mood enhancement, heart health, weight loss, and improved energy. It can also enhance relaxation and promote a better night's sleep. Because it is high in magnesium, it has also been shown to build muscle and aid in muscle recovery. Did you know that cacao also contains more antioxidants than red wine, green tea, and blueberries?

Figs

This dried fruit is high in the calming mineral magnesium, which helps relax the mind and body. Figs are also high in fiber, helping to promote a healthy digestion.

Almonds

This popular nut is high in calcium needed to build strong bones, improve muscle function, and absorb magnesium.

Brazil Nuts

These nuts are high in selenium, a trace mineral essential to immune and thyroid function. Brazil nuts are also high in magnesium which helps with the functioning of muscles, production of protein, and absorption of energy from food.

Superseeds (Flax, Chia, Hemp)

Flaxseeds and chia seeds are high in omega 3s (ALA), which provide antiviral, antifungal, antibacterial, and anticancer properties. Hemp seeds are also high in omega 3s (LA and GLA), along with being high in protein.

Coconut

Coconuts are a healthy saturated fat high in lauric, capric, and caprylic acids, which all have antiviral and antifungal properties contributing to a healthy digestion. Coconuts also contain medium chain fatty acids that can aid in a healthy metabolism.

Leafy Greens

We all know that eating leafy greens provides many benefits, but did you know they are a good source of calcium? Leafy greens are also high in vitamin C, helping to keep your immune system healthy and prevent you from getting sick.

Cod Liver Oil

This omega 3 fat contains EPA and DHA all of which contribute to a healthy heart, brain, hormonal balance, and decreased inflammation. Cod liver oil is also high in vitamin D which is needed to absorb calcium.

Spirulina & Chlorella

This fresh water algae helps to build the immune system, detoxify the body, and improve digestion. Spirulina and chlorella are also high in protein, making it a great source for vegans or protein needs in general.

Maca Powder

This plant powder can boost energy levels and even enhance athletic performance. Maca has also been shown to decrease levels of stress-inducing hormones, cortisol, and adrenaline.

beverages

very berry mineral water cocktail

Serves 4

1 bottle (33.8 ounces) natural sparkling mineral water

8 ounces sparkling juice

1 orange, sliced

1 lemon, sliced

Ice

Combine ingredients in a large pitcher and serve.

tip▶ Skewer raspberries, blueberries, and blackberries on a cocktail straw or toothpick, and place in the freezer overnight. Place frozen fruit skewer in your favorite wine or cocktail glass and add carbonated mineral water.

 Mineral Water Cocktail is full of electrolytes, making it a great sports recovery drink to refuel and replenish the body.

detox juice

Serves 2

Combine all ingredients in a juicer and drink immediately.

1 beet, peeled

2 stalks celery

4 carrots

1 apple, cored

1-inch piece fresh ginger, peeled

 If you are interested in doing a liquid cleanse/detox, try a broth cleanse instead. Simply make your own by boiling chicken/beef bones or buy organic bone broth; heat, and serve with a side of greens. Bone broths contain more vitamins, minerals, and protein compared to traditional broths/stocks.

krazy kale smoothie

Serves 2

Mix all ingredients in a blender until smooth.

2 large kale leaves

2 stalks celery

2 apples, cored

1 cup strawberries, stems removed

1 tablespoon maca powder (optional)

tip ▶ Smoothies don't always have to be made with frozen fruits and vegetables. Stock up at your local Farmer's Market when fresh fruits and veggies are in season!

peanut butter bomb smoothie

Serves 2-3

Mix all ingredients in a blender until smooth.

2 cups almond milk

2 large frozen ripe bananas

1 tablespoon chia seeds

3 tablespoons natural peanut butter

¼ teaspoon vanilla extract

Ice, if desired

 We made this smoothie at one of our retreats and everyone loved it. Nutritious and tasty!

summertime smoothie

Serves 2

Mix all ingredients in a blender until smooth.

1 large nectarine, sliced

½ cup fresh blueberries

1 cup fresh greens like spinach or kale

2 cups coconut water

2 tablespoons almond butter

1 tablespoon chia seeds

1 tablespoon flaxseeds

1 tablespoon shredded coconut

3 ice cubes

tip▶ Hemp seeds are a great alternative to protein powder in your smoothies.

rise & shine smoothie

Serves 3

Mix all ingredients in a blender until smooth.

2 cups water or carrot juice

1 cup kale or spinach

1 banana

2 cups frozen or fresh berries

2 tablespoons chia seeds or ground flaxseeds

2 tablespoons hemp seeds

 Throw flaxseeds or chia seeds into your smoothies for an easy way to add healthy omega 3s to your diet. These super seeds are also high in fiber and protein, and have antiviral properties all contributing to a healthy immune system.

r & r smoothie

Serves 2

Combine all ingredients in a blender until smooth.

1 10-12 ounce bag frozen mixed fruit

1 banana

1 tablespoon cacao nibs

2 cups coconut water

2 dates, pitted (or figs)

2 tablespoons Brazil nuts

2 cups spinach

 Cacao, dates, Brazil nuts, and leafy greens are all high in the calming mineral magnesium, making this a perfect drink for rest and recovery.

homemade coconut milk

Serves 4

Add coconut and water to a blender. Mix on high for 1-2 minutes or until water turns milky. Store in the refrigerator and use within 4 to 5 days. Shake well before using.

1 cup shredded coconut

5-6 cups water

1 teaspoon vanilla extract

 Most store-bought, plant-based milks contain carrageenan, xanthan gum, and other processed stabilizers. You can avoid these types of additives by making your own coconut milk.

molasses & fig almond milk

Serves 5

Place almonds in a glass bowl and cover with water. Soak for 8 hours or overnight. Drain and rinse almonds.

Add almonds, molasses, figs, water, and vanilla extract to blender and mix until smooth.

1 cup raw almonds

1 tablespoon blackstrap molasses

4 dried figs

4 cups water

1 teaspoon vanilla extract (optional)

 Blackstrap molasses and almonds are naturally high in calcium making this a calcium-rich, plant-based milk. One serving provides about 8 grams of protein.

25

breakfasts

oatmeal on the run

Serves 1

Combine dry ingredients in a small travel container and mix to incorporate. Pour almond milk over oat mixture just to cover. Let soak overnight in the refrigerator. Grab and go in the morning.

 chris: My grandmother turned me on to oatmeal when I was 8 years old. She ate it every morning and lived to age 98. I came up with this recipe for those days when I didn't have time to cook oatmeal in the morning. Now it's my favorite way to eat oatmeal.

tip ▶ You can make a big batch to keep in the refrigerator for the week. Play with the combination of fruit and nuts to your liking.

½ cup rolled oats

1 teaspoon ground cinnamon

2 tablespoons raisins

2 tablespoons walnuts (can use any nuts)

⅔ cup almond, coconut, or hemp milk (just enough to cover the oat mixture)

overnight oats with figs & apples

Serves 4

Rinse oats and soak in cold water for 1 hour.

Drain oats and add to small (1.5 quart) slow cooker. Mix in cinnamon and then stir in 4 cups of water, chopped apples or pears, and figs.

Cook in slow cooker for 7-8 hours or overnight. Serve warm with almond milk.

tip ▶ Oat groats are great but who has the time to cook them? Simply throw them in a slow cooker overnight and breakfast is served! The delicious smell will have you out of bed in seconds and this warm bowl of deliciousness will stick with you until lunch.

1 cup oat groats (see page 8 for photo of oat varieties)

1 teaspoon ground cinnamon

4 cups water

1 apple or pear, peeled and chopped

4 dried figs, chopped

superhero breakfast

Serves 8

2 cups traditional quinoa, rinsed and drained

½ cup natural crunchy peanut butter

2 tablespoons honey

1 tablespoon cinnamon

½ cup raisins

Bring quinoa and 4 cups water to a boil.

Lower heat to simmer and cook for 10-15 minutes or until quinoa is al dente, and all the water is absorbed.

While hot, mix in peanut butter, honey, and cinnamon. Stir in raisins.

Serve warm or chilled. Lasts up to 5 days in the refrigerator.

kristen: *I call this a superhero breakfast because it is super healthy and kid-approved!*

 Super-nutrition for a super-hero! Quinoa is an ancient grain high in protein, fiber, and energizing carbohydrates.

traverse city cherry granola

Serves 8-10

3 cups rolled oats

1 cup unsweetened dried coconut flakes

1 cup pecans, roughly chopped

½ cup dried tart cherries

⅛ cup flaxseeds

Dash of sea salt

Dash of nutmeg

½ cup pure maple syrup

¼ cup virgin coconut oil

1 tablespoon honey

1 teaspoon vanilla extract

Preheat oven to 300°F.

Combine the dry ingredients and mix together (oats, coconut flakes, pecans, cherries, flaxseeds, sea salt, and nutmeg).

In a small saucepan, combine the wet ingredients (syrup, virgin coconut oil, honey, and vanilla extract) until melted. Once melted and mixed, pour over the dry ingredients and mix well.

Grease a large cookie sheet with virgin coconut oil. Spread out mixture onto the cookie sheet.

Bake for 15 minutes. Stir mixture on the cookie sheet and bake for another 15 minutes. While still warm, transfer into a large glass container.

holly: *This is a recipe that I perfected using the Target to Table philosophy. I was not always a "Target to Table" girl, but soon after meeting Matt I started challenging myself to make substitutions based on these principles. Now it's second nature for me to adapt all of my recipes.*

 Traverse City, Michigan is known as the cherry capital of the world. With more than 3.8 million tart cherry trees, the Traverse City area produces 70-75% of the tart cherries grown in the United States.

nutzo granola

Serves 8-10

¼ cup chopped pecans

¼ cup sliced almonds or raw almonds

¼ cup sunflower seeds

1 cup steel cut oats

1 tablespoon ground cinnamon

¼ cup virgin coconut oil, melted

¼ cup pure maple syrup

1 tablespoon vanilla extract

¼ cup chia seeds

¼ cup raisins

¼ cup golden raisins

½ cup toasted coconut flakes

Spread pecans, almonds, sunflower seeds, and oats evenly on a baking sheet. Bake for 5 minutes.

Remove tray from oven and place nut and oat mixture in a large mixing bowl. Sprinkle with cinnamon and stir to combine.

Meanwhile, melt virgin coconut oil and mix with maple syrup and vanilla extract. Pour virgin coconut oil syrup over oat mixture and stir to coat.

Spread evenly on a baking sheet and bake in oven for 10 minutes. Stir oat mixture and bake for another 5 minutes.

Remove from oven and pour mixture into a large glass bowl. Add chia seeds, raisins, and toasted coconut, and let cool.

Store in an airtight container and serve with almond milk or organic yogurt.

 Virgin coconut oil is a great substitute for butter or vegetable oil, providing a nutty coconut flavor when added to dishes. This provides a healthy oil + a healthy sweet.

slow cooker blueberry breakfast crisp

Serves 4

Spray the inside of a slow cooker with cooking spray or coat with virgin coconut oil.

Combine blueberries, apple, oats, and cinnamon in a slow cooker. Add in 2 cups of water and cook overnight on low for 7-8 hours.

In a small skillet over medium heat, add virgin coconut oil to melt. Add in almond meal and honey and stir to mix.

Cook for 5 minutes or until almond meal gets slightly toasted. Let sit for 10 minutes.

Serve cooked oats in a small bowl and top with almond meal honey mixture and almond milk if desired.

1 10-ounce package frozen blueberries

1 apple, chopped

1 cup steel cut oats

1 teaspoon cinnamon

2 cups water

For the Topping

1 tablespoon virgin coconut oil

½ cup almond meal (finely ground almonds)

2 tablespoons honey

flax bran muffins

Serves 12

Preheat oven to 350°F.

Combine flour, flaxseeds, oat bran, sugar, agave, baking soda, baking powder, salt, and cinnamon in a large bowl and mix well.

Use a cheese grater to shred carrots and apples. Add carrots, apples, raisins, and nuts.

In a separate bowl, blend egg whites, milk, and vanilla.

Add liquid ingredients to dry ingredients; mix until just combined. Do not overstir.

Coat muffin tin with virgin coconut oil. Divide mixture into 12 muffin cups.

Bake for 25-28 minutes. Allow to cool slightly; remove from muffin tin to finish cooling.

1½ cups white whole wheat flour

¾ cup ground flaxseeds

¾ cup oat bran (use rolled oats and blend in coffee grinder or food processor)

½ cup brown sugar + 1 tablespoon agave nectar

2 teaspoons baking soda

1 teaspoon baking powder

½ teaspoon sea salt

2 teaspoons cinnamon

1½ cups carrots, shredded

2 medium apples, unpeeled, shredded

½ cup raisins

¾ cup chopped walnuts, toasted

3 egg whites (free-range)

¾ cup almond milk

1 teaspoon vanilla extract

tip▶ Make your own oat bran to use in baking by simply blending rolled oats in a food processor.

 This is a favorite recipe from On Target Living: Cooking. Our good friend Bonnie Klinger created it, and we have been proudly sharing it every since.

oatmeal pancakes

Serves 4 (Makes about 10 pancakes)

2 tablespoons almond or coconut milk

5 egg whites

2 large eggs

1½ cups rolled oats

½ cup low-fat cottage cheese

½ cup natural unsweetened applesauce

½ teaspoon vanilla extract

½ teaspoon cinnamon

½ tablespoon virgin coconut oil

Mix all ingredients except oil in a blender until smooth (add more milk for creamier batter).

Pour into large bowl; let stand for 5 minutes.

Pour ⅓ cup batter per pancake onto hot, oiled griddle. Cook until bubbles form, then flip.

Serve topped with a spoonful of fruit, natural applesauce, or pure maple syrup.

matt: *My childhood memories recall weekend breakfasts which always included these pancakes. They were Dad's creation. He always made them on Mother's Day. Guests are always surprised to find out the ingredients. I like to add sliced banana or blueberries to the batter. Oh...and if you haven't done it before, breakfast for dinner is Target to Table approved.*

smoky salmon hash

Serves 4-6

1 (2-pound) salmon fillet, with the skin on

Extra virgin olive oil

6 redskin potatoes, rinsed in water and diced

Sea salt & black pepper

1 large onion, thinly sliced

1 medium red bell pepper, thinly sliced

1 medium yellow bell pepper, thinly sliced

1 small green pepper, thinly sliced

2 cloves garlic, minced

2 green onions, finely chopped

3 sprigs fresh thyme, chopped

1 teaspoon smoked paprika

Pinch cayenne pepper

White vinegar

4 to 6 large eggs

Preheat oven to 350°F.

Place the salmon on a large baking sheet skin-side down. Drizzle salmon with extra virgin olive oil and season with salt and black pepper to taste. Place into the oven and bake for 30 minutes until flaky. Remove from oven and set aside.

Add 2 tablespoons extra virgin olive oil to a large sauté pan over medium-high heat. Add the potatoes and sprinkle with salt and black pepper. Brown on all sides until tender. Transfer potatoes to a large serving bowl.

Add another 2 tablespoons extra virgin olive oil to the sauté pan, and sauté the onions, peppers, garlic, and thyme over medium-high heat. Season with salt, black pepper, smoked paprika, and cayenne pepper and cook until vegetables are tender.

Remove salmon from skin, and crumble it into the hash mixture. Cover to keep warm while you poach the eggs.

To poach eggs, place a large sauté pan over medium heat and fill with a few inches of water. Heat until it simmers. Add a splash of white vinegar. Using a wooden spoon, stir the water in one direction to create a small whirlpool. Add the eggs, one at a time, to the swirling water. Poach to desired doneness. Remove with a slotted spoon.

Serve the poached eggs on top of the hash mixture.

matt: *This dish is our family brunch staple.*

tip ▶ The salmon and potato mixture can be made ahead the day before and reheated in the oven when ready to serve with fresh eggs.

For the crust
(see recipe on page 44)

7 large eggs

½ cup unsweetened coconut milk or milk of choice

½ teaspoon sea salt

¼ teaspoon black pepper

1 cup spinach, chopped

1 red bell pepper, diced

1 tomato, seeds removed and diced

4 ounces feta cheese, crumbled

spinach & feta quiche

Serves 8

Preheat oven to 375°F.

In a large bowl whisk the eggs and milk to combine. Add salt and black pepper, then add the vegetables and feta cheese. Pour the egg mixture into baked pie crust.

Bake for 45 minutes to 1 hour or until fork comes out clean. Let sit 5 minutes before serving.

tip ▶ Adding coconut milk makes the eggs nice and fluffy.

For the crust
(see recipe on page 44)

7 large eggs

½ cup unsweetened coconut milk or milk of choice

½ teaspoon sea salt

¼ teaspoon black pepper

1 10-ounce package California style frozen vegetables, thawed (carrots, cauliflower, zucchini, broccoli)

¼ cup green onions

2 nitrate-free sweet Italian chicken sausages, diced

½ cup raw milk cheddar cheese, shredded

chicken sausage & veggie pie

Serves 8

Preheat oven to 375°F.

In a large bowl whisk the eggs and milk to combine. Add salt and black pepper, then add the vegetables, sausage and cheese. Pour the egg mixture into baked pie shells.

Bake for 45 minutes to 1 hour or until fork comes out clean. Let sit 5 minutes before serving.

oatmeal pie crust

Makes one 9-inch crust

¾ cup rolled oats

½ cup whole wheat flour

¼ teaspoon sea salt

3 tablespoons cold grass-fed butter, cut into small pieces

3 tablespoons coconut milk (or milk of choice)

Preheat oven to 400°F. Coat a 9-inch pie dish with extra virgin olive oil.

Put the oats, flour, and salt in the bowl of a food processor and pulse to combine. Add the butter and pulse until you get a pebbly texture. Add the milk to combine.

Form the mixture into a ball and place between two sheets of floured waxed paper. Roll into a 10-inch circle. Remove the top sheet of waxed paper and flip the crust side onto the pie dish.

Gently remove the second layer of waxed paper, and press the crust into the corners of the dish. Fold over any crust that overlaps the edge of the dish.

Bake for 10 minutes and then remove to cool before adding egg mixture.

tip ▶ To save time in the kitchen, you may use a frozen organic pie crust from the grocery store.

asparagus & parmesan frittata

Serves 6-8

Preheat oven to 350°F.

Whisk all ingredients together in a mixing bowl.

Spray extra virgin olive oil on a mini muffin pan and fill each spot with the egg mixture.

Cook for 8-10 minutes or until cooked through. Serve immediately.

6 free-range eggs

1 cup almond or coconut milk

¼ cup fresh Parmesan cheese

½ cup small asparagus, chopped

½ teaspoon sea salt

¼ teaspoon black pepper

 These little bundles are light and fluffy. This is an elegant way to make a breakfast item that isn't full of high fat ingredients.

snacks

roasted spiced chickpeas

Serves 4

2 cans chickpeas

1 tablespoon extra virgin olive oil

1 teaspoon cumin

1 teaspoon chili powder

¼ teaspoon cayenne pepper

½ teaspoon sea salt

Preheat oven to 350°F.

Drain and rinse 2 cans of chickpeas and pat dry with paper towel.

Mix with 1 tablespoon extra virgin olive oil and spices.

Spread on parchment lined baking sheet and bake for 45-50 minutes, stirring frequently.

They will dry and become crunchy. Watch carefully so they don't burn.

kale chips

1 bunch kale, stems removed, then chopped

1 tablespoon extra virgin olive oil

Sea salt & black pepper to taste

Preheat oven to 350°F.

Toss kale with extra virgin olive oil, salt, and black pepper. Spread evenly in one layer on a large cookie sheet.

Place on middle rack in the oven.

Stir and flip frequently until the kale is crunchy and golden brown, approximately 20-25 min.

The kale will initially wilt, but will then start to dry and crisp. Watch carefully.

 This is a yummy guilt-free chip!

travel trail mix

Serves 2

Combine ingredients in a small sandwich bag to take on the go.

chris: *I created this snack out of desperation. I found myself stuck in the airport with very few healthy food options. If you find yourself sitting next to me on an airplane, I might share my stash with you.* ☺

1 tablespoon cacao nibs

2 Turkish figs

½ cup rolled oats

¼ cup raw macadamia nuts or nuts of choice

2 tablespoons raisins

2 tablespoons shredded coconut

coconut oil kettle corn

Serves 2

Heat coconut oil in saucepan. Drop 2 popcorn kernels in oil and wait until kernels pop. Once popped, add in the rest of the kernels and cover with a tight fitting lid.

Pop for 2-3 minutes or until the popping noise stops.

While popcorn is hot, stir in 1 tablespoon of agave nectar, a sprinkle of cinnamon, and sea salt to taste.

1 tablespoon virgin coconut oil

¼ cup corn kernels

1 tablespoon agave nectar

Cinnamon for sprinkling

Sea salt to taste

tip▶ Leave out the agave and cinnamon for a traditional popcorn taste.

 A healthy alternative to theatre-style popcorn.

honey flax energy bites

Makes 30

2 cups rolled oats

1 cup natural peanut butter

½ cup raw honey

1 cup ground flaxseeds

1 teaspoon vanilla extract

1 tablespoon virgin coconut oil

Optional add-ins:

    dark chocolate chips

    organic shredded coconut

    cacao nibs

Mix all ingredients together.

Coat hands with virgin coconut oil and form batter into small balls.

Store in refrigerator for 1 hour before serving. Freezes well.

 So amazingly delicious you may even reintroduce this recipe as a healthy dessert.

apricot almond coconut bars

Makes 8 (4-inch) bars

In a food processor, add apricots and blend until puréed.

Add in almond butter, rolled oats, coconut, and vanilla extract.

Blend until mixture forms a thick paste.

Place mixture in a small, square cake pan. Press to mold into pan.

Freeze for 20 minutes and cut into small bars.

Bars can be stored in the refrigerator for 1-2 weeks or in the freezer for up to 3 months.

1 12-ounce bag dried apricots

¾ cup almond butter

½ cup rolled oats

1 cup toasted raw coconut

1 tablespoon vanilla extract

 This is a great alternative to the highly processed food bars found in most grocery stores.

homemade applesauce

Serves 4-6

3 pounds (10-12) small apples, cored and peeled

1 tablespoon ground cinnamon or 2 cinnamon sticks

1 teaspoon vanilla extract

Cut cored apples into large wedges and combine all ingredients in a large slow cooker. Cook on low for 4-6 hours or high for 2-3 hours.

"When life gives you apples, make applesauce."

 For added fiber, leave the skin on the apples

buffalo cauliflower

Serves 6

1 cup water

1 cup white whole wheat flour

½ teaspoon sea salt

1 tablespoon garlic powder

1 head of cauliflower, broken into small florets

1 bottle of hot sauce

1 tablespoon butter, melted

Preheat oven to 450°F.

Lightly spray a large nonstick baking sheet with oil.

Combine water, flour, salt, and garlic powder in a large bowl, and stir until well mixed.

Add the cauliflower pieces to the flour mixture and coat well.

Transfer coated cauliflower to baking sheet and bake for 20 minutes.

Meanwhile, combine the hot sauce and butter in a small bowl.

Pour hot sauce mixture over the baked cauliflower and continue baking for another 5 minutes.

Serve with your favorite ranch dressing or blue cheese dip and celery sticks for a guilt-free tailgate dish!

tip ▶ See Ranch Dressing recipe, page 98.

sean's guaca-money

Serves 6

3 avocados

½ cup sweet onions, chopped

1 cup tomatoes, chopped

Juice of 1 lime

½ teaspoon sea salt

½ teaspoon pepper

2 cloves garlic, minced (optional)

1 bunch cilantro, finely chopped (optional)

Peel and chop avocado, and place in large mixing bowl.

Crush avocados with a fork.

Add in the remaining ingredients and mix to combine.

sean: *I won Kristen's heart with this money recipe.*

layered greek dip

Serves 4-6

1 pound ground bison, beef, or chicken

1 tablespoon herbes de Provence or Greek seasoning

1 teaspoon garlic powder

½ teaspoon cinnamon

Sea salt and pepper to taste

1 cup hummus (see recipe page 57)

½ red onion, diced

1 cup tzatziki sauce (see recipe page 134)

½ cup cucumbers, diced

½ cup tomatoes, diced

½ cup pitted Kalamata olives, chopped

½ cup feta cheese, crumbled

¼ cup fresh parsley, chopped

Heat a large skillet over medium-high heat and add in 1 tablespoon extra virgin olive oil. Add ground meat and seasoning, and cook until browned.

In a shallow (10x6 inch) baking dish spread each ingredient in a single layer in this order: hummus, ground meat, red onion, tzatziki, cucumbers, tomatoes, olives, feta, and parsley.

Serve immediately or refrigerate until ready to eat. Serve with pita chips.

lebanese hummus

Serves 4

Place all ingredients except water into a food processor.

Blend 2-3 minutes while pouring in water until desired consistency.

Place in bowl and drizzle with extra virgin olive oil. Toasted pine nuts and paprika can also be added.

Serve with pita bread or veggie sticks.

2 garlic cloves, peeled and pressed

1 can chickpeas, drained and rinsed

1 cup tahini

Juice of 1 lemon, may need to add more lemon to taste

1 teaspoon sea salt

⅓ cup water or more as needed for desired consistency

soups

chicken pot pie soup

Serves 4-6 (pictured on page 58)

For the soup:

2 tablespoons extra virgin olive oil

3 medium carrots, sliced

3 stalks celery, sliced

2-3 redskin potatoes, peeled and cubed

2 cups mushrooms, diced

2 cloves garlic, minced

½ large yellow onion, diced

2 chicken breasts, cubed

Sea salt & black pepper

Onion powder

Garlic powder

Dried thyme

¾ cup frozen peas

1 pack concentrated chicken stock or 1 tablespoon chicken soup base

16 ounces chicken stock

1 container organic cream of chicken soup

1 bay leaf

For the "crust:"

1 large russet potato, sliced thin with a mandolin (6 slices per serving bowl)

 When using store-bought soups, choose organic.

To make the soup:

In large Dutch oven, heat extra virgin olive oil over medium heat.

Add all the chopped vegetables except the frozen peas to the pan and cook for 2-3 minutes until the vegetables start to become tender.

Season the cubed chicken with garlic powder, sea salt, black pepper, onion powder, and thyme. Add the chicken to the vegetables in the pan and cook for another 5 minutes. Do not overcook the chicken as it will become dry.

Add the peas, concentrated chicken stock or soup base, and 16 ounces of chicken stock to the pot.

Add 1 teaspoon of thyme, bay leaf and 1 tablespoon of sea salt, and cook over medium low heat uncovered for 30 minutes.

After 30 minutes, add the cream of chicken soup and stir. Heat for 3 minutes on medium heat and let cool to serving temperature.

To make the "crust:"

Potato slices serve as the upper crust. While everything is cooking, thinly slice the russet potato. You will need about 6 slices per individual serving.

Lightly oil a large sheet pan. Lay the slices of potato in a pinwheel pattern. Repeat for as many individuals you plan to serve. Sprinkle the tops of the potato pinwheels with extra virgin olive oil and season with salt and black pepper. Bake in 350°F oven for about 30 minutes until lightly browned.

Serve in individual bowls and top with potato pinwheels.

south of the border chicken corn chowder

matt: *I made this soup for the family and forgot to remove the jalapeño seeds. Needless to say, they were pretty hot under the collar.*

Serves 6

Place chicken and celery in a medium sauce pan. Fill with enough water to cover chicken. Add ½ teaspoon sea salt. Cook for 20-25 minutes. Remove chicken from broth to cool. Using two forks, pull chicken apart into bite-size pieces.

Meanwhile, boil cubed potatoes in a separate pot until al dente. Remove from water and set aside.

Turn oven on high broil. Slice 2 of the Roma tomatoes in half lengthwise. Place the tomatoes and peppers in a single layer on ½ of a large baking sheet. Place 2 cups of corn on the remaining half of baking sheet. Drizzle with extra virgin olive oil and season with sea salt and black pepper. Broil for 10 minutes then turn the tomatoes and peppers, and toss the corn. Return to broil for another 10 more minutes, watching carefully not to burn the vegetables but allowing them to get a slight char.

Once cooled, remove the skin of the tomatoes. Set aside one cup roasted corn for later.

Place 1 cup of the chicken broth, roasted tomatoes, peppers, and 1 cup of corn into the blender. Blend for 10-15 seconds.

In Dutch oven heat 1 tablespoon of extra virgin olive oil over medium heat. Add onions and garlic, and cook for 3 minutes. Add the pulled chicken, onion powder and sriracha chili sauce. Cook for 3 minutes. Add 2 cups chicken broth and continue to cook for 5 minutes. Add the blended liquid, potatoes, and reserved roasted corn. Chop the remaining 2 Roma tomatoes and add them to the soup. Cover the soup and simmer for 20 minutes.

Serve with sliced avocado and tortilla chips on top.

2 boneless, skinless chicken breasts

3 celery stalks

½ teaspoon sea salt

1½ cups cubed potatoes, skin on

4 Roma tomatoes

1 red pepper, washed and quartered

1 green pepper, washed and quartered

½ jalapeño, sliced lengthwise and seeds removed

2 cups frozen corn, thawed

3 cups chicken broth

½ yellow onion, diced

3 cloves of garlic, diced

2 teaspoons sriracha chili sauce

1 teaspoon onion powder

Extra virgin olive oil

Sea salt & black pepper to taste

Garnish with sliced avocado and blue corn tortilla chips

mom's chicken noodle soup

Serves 10-12

Clean chicken and place it whole in an 8-quart soup pot. Cover with fresh water. Add whole carrots, celery, 2 onions, sea salt, peppercorns, bay leaf, whole allspice, and stick cinnamon. Bring to a boil and then lower heat to simmer gently for 1 hour, until chicken is tender and broth is developed.

Remove chicken and set aside to cool. Strain broth, clean soup pot, and return strained broth to pot. Taste broth to determine if additional sea salt and/or black pepper is necessary and add to taste.

Add remaining vegetables except spinach or kale to the broth in the pot. Gently simmer for 20-30 minutes until vegetables are tender.

Meanwhile, cook pasta or rice, drain, and set aside.

After the vegetables in the broth are tender, add spinach or kale and simmer an additional 5 minutes.

Remove skin from chicken and chicken from the bone. Cut chicken into bite-sized pieces and return all the chicken to the soup pot. Add pasta or rice and heat for another 10 minutes.

Enjoy!

paula: *I was honored that my kids asked me to put my chicken soup recipe in their cookbook. Actually, this is my mom's chicken soup recipe, but we all love it. What hits the spot better than a bowl of homemade chicken noodle soup?*

For the broth:

1 whole chicken (3-4 pounds)

2 whole carrots

2 stalks celery with leaves

2 small-sized onions, peeled, whole

2 tablespoons coarse sea salt

1 tablespoon whole peppercorns

1 bay leaf

1 tablespoon whole allspice

2 sticks cinnamon

For the soup:

2 cups carrots, chopped

2 cups celery, chopped

1 pound mushrooms, sliced

6 small-sized onions, peeled, left whole

4 cups cooked egg noodles (or your favorite pasta or rice)

2 cups baby spinach or chopped kale

tip ▶ Cinnamon and allspice are the secret ingredients that make this soup taste like mom's.

wild rice soup with mushrooms & pesto

Serves 6-8

For the chicken stock:

1 whole chicken

5 large carrots, washed not peeled, rough chopped in 3-inch pieces

5 large celery stalks washed, rough chopped in 3-inch pieces

1 large onion, washed not peeled, cut into 4 pieces

1 tablespoon peppercorns

2 tablespoons sea salt

10 stalks thyme

1 large stalk rosemary

Handful fresh parsley

For the soup:

3 large carrots, peeled and sliced

1 pint mushrooms, sliced

2 cups cooked wild rice

2 cups baby spinach

For the pesto:

1 cup walnuts

4 cups fresh basil

1 cup spinach

2 tablespoons extra virgin olive oil

3 cloves garlic

1 teaspoon sea salt

To make the chicken stock:

Place all the ingredients in a large pot and fill with water (2 inches above the ingredients).

Bring to a boil and simmer for 1-2 hours or until the broth is golden and the chicken is cooked.

Strain the broth into a large soup pot.

Dispose of the veggies and set chicken aside.

Add the carrots and mushrooms to the pot of fresh chicken broth. Cook until vegetables are tender.

Add the cooked rice and spinach, and continue to cook until rice is warm and spinach is wilted.

Meanwhile, remove the skin from the chicken and remove all of the meat. Cut it into bite size pieces and toss into soup.

To make pesto:

Put all the pesto ingredients except the oil in a food processor, start the food processor, and then drizzle in the oil until well combined.

Add the pesto to the soup. Season with additional sea salt and black pepper to taste and serve.

tip ▶ This chicken stock can be made in advance and frozen for any recipe that calls for chicken stock. The chicken can be used for other recipes like the Awesome Chicken Salad on page 108.

white bean chicken chili

Serves 4

Cut chicken into bite sized pieces and season with salt and black pepper.

Heat oil in a large saucepot over medium-high heat. Add chicken and heat until cooked through and juices run clear.

Add in beans, salsa, and broth. Cook until heated through.

Sprinkle with cheddar and top with crumbled corn chips.

Serve and enjoy while you watch your favorite game!

1 pound boneless, skinless chicken breasts

1 tablespoon extra virgin olive oil

1 48-ounce jar great northern beans, drained and rinsed

1 24-ounce jar corn and black bean salsa

2 cups chicken broth

Garnish with 1 cup shredded cheddar cheese and 2 cups crumbled blue corn chips

kristen: *This was a staple meal when I was a broke college student living with 8 girls at WMU! Go Broncos!*

tip ▶ To make this a dip just leave out the chicken broth. The recipe doubles and freezes well.

cook-off chili

Serves 4-6

10 ounces ground bison or turkey

1 cup onion, chopped

1 cup green pepper, chopped

2 teaspoons garlic, minced

1 15-ounce can kidney, black, or pinto beans, rinsed and drained

1 14.5-ounce can stewed tomatoes

1 8-ounce can tomato sauce

1 cup beef, chicken, or vegetable broth

½ cup filtered water

½ cup frozen corn

½ tablespoon chili powder

½ teaspoon cumin

½ teaspoon dried oregano

1 teaspoon fresh cilantro

Sea salt & black pepper, to taste

Garnish with avocado, onion, tomato, and/or cheese

Heat extra virgin olive oil in a 4-quart sauce pan over medium heat.

Brown ground meat in sauce pan.

Add onions, green pepper, and garlic. Heat until vegetables are tender and slightly browned.

Add remaining ingredients and simmer for 30 minutes.

Sprinkle with chopped avocado, onion, tomato, and/or cheese to serve.

tip ▶ Can be made a day ahead and can be frozen for up to 3 months.

 A big part of our On Target Living program is teaching people how to feel and perform their best in work and in life. We conduct live, multi-day retreats that immerse attendees into the program. One of our retreat events is a team chili cook-off. Teams combine ingredients and flavors to make their own signature chili recipe. Judges choose the winners on taste, appearance, and creativity.

bison stew

Serves 6

Heat extra virgin olive oil over medium-high heat in a 6-quart saucepan.

Brown bison, then add onion and garlic, and cook until onions are soft.

Add remaining ingredients and simmer for 30 minutes or until vegetables are tender.

Let sit 10 minutes before serving.

Season with sea salt and black pepper to taste.

1 tablespoon extra virgin olive oil

1 pound ground bison

1 onion, chopped

3 cloves garlic, diced

1 tablespoon herbes de Provence

4 stalks celery, chopped

3 large parsnips, peeled and chopped

3 large carrots, peeled and chopped

1 pound button mushrooms, sliced

1 can Italian seasoned diced tomatoes

2 quarts chicken broth

½ head cabbage, sliced

2 cups kale, chopped

Sea salt & black pepper to taste

 Wild game, such as rabbit, pheasant, goose, duck, deer, bear, elk, and bison, consume a more natural diet. Their meat tends to have a lower fat content and contain more anti-inflammatory omega-3s than conventional meats.

italian zuppa

Serves 4-6

1 pound sweet Italian sausage

3 slices nitrate-free organic bacon

1 tablespoon Italian seasoning

1 onion, diced

2 cloves garlic, minced

7 cups chicken broth

1 cup water

4 large yellow potatoes, cut in half lengthwise and sliced thin

2 cups kale, chopped

Pinch of red pepper

Sea salt & black pepper to taste

½ cup organic half and half

Heat a large soup pot on medium-high heat.

Add sausage and bacon, and cook until sausage is cooked through and bacon is crispy.

Add Italian seasoning and stir to mix.

Add in onion and garlic, and cook until tender.

Add broth and water, and bring to a boil.

Add in sliced potatoes, and cook over medium heat for 5-10 minutes or until potatoes are al dente.

Add in kale, red pepper, and sea salt and black pepper to taste.

Turn off heat and stir in half and half.

Serve hot with fresh baked bread and parmesan cheese.

kristen: *I owe this creation to the influence of my BFF Annie. We have so many memories and delicious creations from our days in the Johnson kitchen.*

tomato basil soup

Serves 4-6

Heat extra virgin olive oil in a heavy-bottomed soup pot.

Sauté onion until soft and translucent, 3-5 minutes.

Add garlic and sauté until fragrant, 1 minute.

Add tomatoes, tomato paste, broth, dried basil, black pepper, and sea salt. Bring to a boil, reduce to a simmer and cook 10 minutes.

Stir in fresh basil and serve.

2 teaspoons extra virgin olive oil

1 medium onion, finely chopped

4 garlic cloves, minced

2 28-ounce cans crushed tomatoes

1 tablespoon tomato paste

2 ½ cups chicken broth

½ teaspoon dried basil

1 teaspoon coarse black pepper

2 teaspoons sea salt

20 leaves fresh basil, torn or coarsely chopped

very veggie soup

Serves 6-8

1 tablespoon extra virgin olive oil

1 yellow onion, chopped

3 cloves garlic, minced

1-inch fresh ginger, minced

2 cups celery, chopped

2 cups carrots, chopped

2 leeks, cleaned and chopped - using white parts only

5 sprigs fresh thyme

1 bay leaf

2 cups zucchini, diced

1 cup green cabbage, chopped

1 bunch Swiss chard or any greens of choice, stems remove and leaves chopped

8 cups vegetable broth

Heat oil in a large soup pot. Add in onion, garlic, ginger, celery, carrots, leeks, thyme, and bay leaf and simmer until vegetables are slightly tender, about 5 minutes. Season to taste with salt and black pepper.

Add in zucchini, cabbage, Swiss chard, and broth. Stir to mix and simmer for 10-15 minutes until vegetables are tender. Season again with salt and black pepper to taste.

tip ▶ To make it heartier, throw in cooked quinoa, farro, or any grain of choice.

 Give the body proper fuel, rest, and exercise, and it will naturally detoxify itself. There is no magic "juice" detox.

Chewing whole foods that are loaded with vitamins, minerals, antioxidants, protein, and fiber will help to stimulate digestive enzymes that assist with digestion and keep you feeling full and satisfied.

Why guzzle hundreds of calories worth of fruit when you can eat one serving of soup and actually feel full?

"fungi" mushroom soup

Serves 4

3 tablespoons extra virgin olive oil

10 ounces mushrooms of your choice, washed and chopped

1 yellow onion, chopped

2 garlic cloves, chopped

2 cups chicken broth

2 cups skim milk

8 ounces button mushrooms, washed and chopped

Sea salt & black pepper to taste

Garnish with fresh basil

Add 2 tablespoons extra virgin olive oil to a large soup pot. Sauté 10 ounces of mushrooms along with onions and garlic until the onions are translucent.

Add chicken broth and milk, and slowly bring to a boil. Cool for 5 minutes.

Carefully put all ingredients in blender and pulse for 30 seconds until puréed.

In a deep pan, sauté the button mushrooms in 1 tablespoon of extra virgin olive oil for 5 minutes.

Add the puréed soup.

Sprinkle with fresh basil.

 Mushrooms are high in energizing B vitamins and choline, which help fight inflammation. Mushrooms are also especially high in selenium, an antioxidant-rich mineral that helps strengthen the immune system and fight disease. Did you know that mushrooms are the only plant-based source of vitamin D?

coconut ginger soup

Serves 4

In a small skillet cook mushrooms covered on medium-low heat until all the liquid has evaporated. Set aside.

In a large soup pot cook jalapeño and ginger in 1 tablespoon extra virgin olive oil over medium heat until tender.

Add in chicken broth, coconut milk, and Bragg's Liquid Aminos, and heat to a low boil. Do not over boil because the coconut milk will burn.

Add in ¾ of package of noodles and cook until al dente.

Add in reserved mushrooms, bamboo shoots, and green onions, and turn off heat.

Let soup sit for 5 minutes before serving.

Season with salt and black pepper to taste if needed. Top with fresh parsley.

Serve with a fork and a spoon.

1 pint mushrooms, sliced thin

1 small jalapeño pepper, seeds removed and diced

1 tablespoon ginger, grated with a microplane

1 quart chicken broth

1 can unsweetened coconut milk

⅓ cup Bragg's Liquid Aminos

1 package noodles (brown rice, soba, or udon)

1 small container bamboo shoots

½ cup green onions, sliced

Garnish with fresh parsley

This is a gourmet and healthy "ramen noodle soup."

i love butternut squash soup

Serves 4-6

In an 8-quart soup pot, melt butter and oil together over medium-high heat. Add the onion, carrot, apple, and garlic, and sauté for about 5 minutes until the vegetables are soft.

Add the squash and the chicken stock. Bring mixture to a boil.

Add sage and lower to simmer for about 30 minutes until squash is tender.

Turn off the heat to cool slightly. Using a blender, food processor or immersion blender, blend the mixture until smooth and thick. Season with sea salt and black pepper.

Serve warm topped with toasted pumpkin seeds and fried sage leaves if desired.

2 tablespoons butter

2 tablespoons extra virgin olive oil

1 medium onion, chopped

1 medium carrot, peeled and chopped

1 medium apple, peeled and chopped

3 cloves garlic, minced

1 large butternut squash, peeled, seeded and cut into 1-inch pieces (about 8 cups)

6 cups chicken stock

Sea salt & black pepper to taste

¼ cup chopped fresh sage leaves

Garnish with ¼ cup toasted pumpkin seeds and 6 lightly fried fresh sage leaves

salads

dressings

mediterranean salad

Serves 4 (pictured on page 80)

Combine salad ingredients in a large bowl.

Toss with **Herb & Red Wine Vinaigrette** below.

Crumble toasted pita chips on top of salad for a little crunch.

1 small package baby spinach

2 heads romaine lettuce

1 can chickpeas, drained and rinsed

¼ cup feta cheese, crumbled

½ cup cherry tomatoes, halved

¼ cup pitted Kalamata olives or black olives

½ cup carrots, shredded

½ red onion, diced

1 large beet, boiled and sliced, or 1 can sliced beets

Pita chips

herb & red wine vinaigrette

Mix together dressing ingredients and toss into salad mixture.

½ cup red wine vinegar

½ cup extra virgin olive oil

1 teaspoon Dijon mustard

2 garlic cloves, diced

2 tablespoons fresh basil, chopped

1 tablespoon fresh parsley, chopped

¼ teaspoon honey

Sea salt & black pepper to taste

 Store-bought dressings can be expensive and unhealthy. Save money by making your own homemade versions with better ingredients.

taco salad

Serves 4

Brown ground meat in extra virgin olive oil over medium-high heat.

Add taco seasoning and water, and heat for 2 minutes or until liquid is absorbed.

Add the rest of the vegetable ingredients to the ground meat and toss into lettuce.

Toss with **Southwest Yogurt Dressing** below.

Top with cheese, salsa, guacamole, and crushed tortilla chips.

tip▶ If you are short on time or want something easier, find an organic taco seasoning mix and use ½ packet for the meat mixture and ½ packet for the dressing.

southwest yogurt dressing

Combine dressing ingredients and toss into salad.

 Greek yogurt contains twice the protein of regular yogurt and less lactose.

Salad:

1 pound lean ground turkey, bison, or beef

1 tablespoon extra virgin olive oil

1 tablespoon Taco Seasoning (see recipe below)

¼ cup water

3 heads romaine lettuce, chopped

1 red bell pepper, chopped

1 small red onion, diced

1 can black beans, drained and rinsed

1 can corn, drained

Taco Seasoning:

1 tablespoon chili powder

1½ teaspoon cumin powder

¼ teaspoon garlic powder

¼ teaspoon onion powder

¼ teaspoon dried oregano

¼ teaspoon paprika

1 teaspoon sea salt

1 teaspoon black pepper

Pinch, cayenne pepper

1 6-ounce container plain Greek yogurt

¼ cup coconut milk

1 tablespoon Taco Seasoning

superfoods salad

Serves 6

Combine salad ingredients and toss in a large bowl.

Pour **Pomegranate Dressing** below over salad and toss to coat.

Refrigerate for 1 hour before serving.

Store in the refrigerator for up to 3 days.

1 bunch kale, stems removed and chopped

½ cup frozen, shelled edamame, thawed

1 pint blueberries, washed and drained

¼ cup pumpkin seeds

¼ cup walnuts, chopped

¼ cup goji berries

½ red onion, diced

3 large carrots, peeled and diced

2 tablespoons chia seeds

 Throw chia seeds and goji berries on top of a salad for a burst of flavor and nutrition.

pomegranate dressing

Combine dressing ingredients and mix well.

½ cup pure pomegranate juice

¼ cup extra virgin olive oil

1 tablespoon red wine vinegar

1 teaspoon ground turmeric

Sea salt & black pepper to taste

 Once in a while you can make Sunday a Salad Sunday night. It's a new way to reintroduce salads for dinner! After a long weekend of eating out and going out with friends, this may be exactly what you need to get back on your Target to Table track.

gyro greek salad

Serves 4

1 pound ground lamb, beef, or bison

2 tablespoons extra virgin olive oil

1 tablespoon Greek seasoning or ½ teaspoon dried oregano and ½ teaspoon dried mint

Sea salt and black pepper to taste

2 heads romaine lettuce, chopped

¼ cup pitted Kalamata olives

½ red onion, diced

1 small cucumber, peeled and diced

½ cup cherry tomatoes, halved

¼ cup feta cheese, crumbled

¼ cup pine nuts, toasted

Heat 1 tablespoon extra virgin olive oil in a large skillet over medium-high heat.

Cook ground meat and Greek seasoning until cooked through. Season with sea salt and black pepper.

Toss with **Greek Yogurt Dressing** below to coat.

Add remaining ingredients and top with ground meat and toasted pine nuts.

 Use extra virgin olive oil for cooking. Extra virgin means it is the first press of the olive retaining the most flavor and nutrition.

greek yogurt dressing

1 cup plain Greek yogurt

2 tablespoons red wine vinegar

1 tablespoon dried dill weed

1 tablespoon oregano

2 cloves garlic, minced

Sea salt & black pepper to taste

Combine dressing ingredients in a large bowl and stir to mix.

warm butternut & chickpea salad

Serves 4

Preheat oven to 425°F.

In large bowl, combine the butternut squash, garlic, olive oil, and a few pinches of sea salt. Toss the squash pieces until evenly coated.

Roast them on a baking sheet for 25 minutes, or until soft. Remove from the oven and cool.

To assemble the salad, combine the squash, chickpeas, onion, and cilantro or parsley in a large salad bowl.

Toss with **Tahini Dressing** below or serve dressing on the side.

Serve immediately.

1 medium butternut squash (2 to 2.5 pounds), peeled, seeded, and cut into 1½-inch pieces

1 medium garlic clove, minced or pressed

2 tablespoons extra virgin olive oil

Sea salt

1 15-ounce can chickpeas, drained and rinsed

¼ medium red onion, finely chopped

¼ cup fresh cilantro or parsley, chopped

tahini dressing

Combine the garlic and lemon juice in a small mixing bowl. Add the tahini and whisk to blend.

Gradually whisk in the olive oil and water until the dressing is combined. Add additional water to achieve desired consistency.

1 medium garlic clove, finely minced with a pinch of sea salt

¼ cup lemon juice

3 tablespoons tahini, well stirred

2 tablespoons water

2 tablespoons olive oil, plus more to taste

 Tahini is a paste made from ground, hulled sesame seeds and used in North African, Greek, Turkish, and Middle Eastern cuisine. Tahini is a major component in hummus and baba ghanoush. It adds a creamy texture when used in salad dressings.

mexican kale salad

Serves 4

1 can vegetarian refried beans

1 bag tortilla chips

1 pound cheddar cheese, shredded

1 pound boneless, skinless chicken breasts

1 cup chicken broth

1 package taco seasoning (see page 83 for homemade Taco Seasoning recipe)

1 6-ounce package baby kale

½ cup green onions, chopped

½ cup frozen peas, thawed

¼ cup parmesan cheese, shredded

1 tomato, diced

Guacamole (see Guaca-money recipe on page 56)

 Remember to choose organic animal products (cheese, chicken, etc.) and organic corn products when available.

Preheat oven to 350°F.

Place refried beans in a small casserole dish and cover with foil. Place in oven to warm for 10-15 minutes.

Lay tortilla chips evenly on a large baking sheet. Using a spoon or spatula, spread warm refried beans on tortilla chips and top with cheddar cheese. Bake for 10-12 minutes or until cheese is melted.

Meanwhile, poach chicken breasts in chicken broth until tender. Leaving the chicken in the cooking liquid, set aside to cool slightly. Once chicken has cooled a bit, remove from liquid and shred by pulling meat apart with two forks.

Place shredded chicken in a skillet and add taco seasoning mixed with ¼ cup of warm water. Heat until chicken is warmed and liquid is absorbed, about 2-3 minutes.

For the salad, mix baby kale, green onions, peas, parmesan, tomatoes, and shredded chicken together in a large salad bowl. Toss with enough **Apple Cider Vinaigrette** below to coat the greens.

Remove tortilla chips from oven and evenly spread guacamole over chips.

Top tortilla chips with salad mixture and serve.

apple cider vinaigrette

1 cup raw apple cider vinegar

½ cup extra virgin olive oil

Sea salt & black pepper to taste

Whisk dressing ingredients and pour over salad (may not need all of dressing depending on the size of salad). Toss to mix.

5 taste salad

Serving 4

Rinse lentil and rice mixture.

Combine lentil mixture and broth in a small saucepan. Bring to a boil, cover, and reduce to a low simmer for 30 minutes until lentils are tender and liquid is absorbed. Remove from heat and let cool for 10 minutes.

Add baby kale to a large mixing bowl and coat with **5 Taste Vinaigrette** below.

Add lentil and rice mixture to baby kale. The warmed mixture will soften the baby kale so that the kale has a slightly wilted look.

Add the rest of the ingredients and toss to mix.

Serve immediately and enjoy the **5 tastes** of eating right!

1 cup Lentil Soup Mix (or a mixture of ¼ cup each green lentils, red lentils, black lentils, and brown rice)

2 cups chicken broth

1 package baby kale **(bitter)**

1 package shiitake mushrooms, sautéed **(umami)**

2 medium-sized beets, peeled and boiled until tender **(sweet)**

¼ cup red onion, diced

3 stalks celery, diced **(salty)**

¼ cup dried or fresh blueberries **(sour)**

5 taste vinaigrette

Combine vinaigrette ingredients in a small bowl and set aside.

¼ cup fig balsamic vinegar

¼ cup extra virgin olive oil

1 teaspoon curry powder

 There are five types of receptors on the tongue that sense the flavors we taste. They are sour, sweet, salty, bitter, and umami. Did you know that umami is a Japanese word that describes a meaty or savory taste? Blending these tastes together is the foundation for great tasting recipes. See page 9 for more information on the 5 tastes.

tip ▶ Infuse your own vinegar by soaking a couple chopped figs in balsamic vinegar for 1 hour.

garbage chopped salad

Serves 4

Combine all salad ingredients and toss with **Herb & Red Wine Vinaigrette** below.

3 hearts romaine lettuce, diced

2 Roma tomatoes, chopped

1 green bell pepper, diced

½ red onion, chopped

½ cup pitted Kalamata olives

1 4-ounce roll Italian salami, chopped into ½-inch pieces

1 4-ounce provolone cheese, chopped into ½-inch pieces

1 can artichokes, drained and sliced

1 can hearts of palm, drained and chopped

tip ▶ This garbage salad or "kitchen-sink" recipe was created by adding a hodgepodge of ingredients to make a creation that just works.

herb & red wine vinaigrette

Mix together dressing ingredients and toss into salad mixture.

½ cup red wine vinegar

½ cup extra virgin olive oil

1 teaspoon Dijon mustard

2 garlic cloves, diced

2 tablespoons fresh basil, chopped

1 tablespoon fresh parsley, chopped

¼ teaspoon honey

Sea salt & black pepper to taste

wheat berry salad

Serve 4-6

1 cup wheat berries, rinsed and drained

3½ cups water

¼ cup balsamic vinegar

¼ cup extra virgin olive oil

Sea salt & black pepper to taste

1 tablespoon fresh chopped basil

½ cup dried cherries

¼ cup green onions, chopped

¼ cup parsley, chopped

Garnish with ¼ cup each pomegranate seeds, crumbled goat cheese and pumpkin seeds

Add wheat berries and water to small soup pot. Bring to a boil over high heat. Reduce heat to low, cover and cook for 1 hour until wheat berries are cooked and liquid is absorbed. Let cool for 10 minutes.

Add balsamic, oil, salt, black pepper, and basil to the cooled wheat berries. Stir to mix.

Add cherries, onions, parsley and stir to combine.

Chill in refrigerator overnight or serve immediately.

Top with pomegranate seeds, goat cheese, and pumpkin seeds.

 Did you know wheatgrass comes from the wheat berry?

quinoa salad with pistachios & cranberries

Serves 4

Toast the quinoa in a 4-quart pot over high heat, shaking the pan occasionally, until the quinoa is light brown, starts to crackle, and smells a bit toasted, about 5 minutes.

Add the water to the toasted quinoa, cover and bring to a simmer. Cook until the quinoa is soft but still has a little bite, about 15 minutes. The water should be totally absorbed.

Transfer quinoa to a bowl and let cool slightly. Once the quinoa has cooled, add the pistachio nuts, celery, scallions, and cranberries, and toss everything together.

Dress the salad with the **Dijon Mustard Vinaigrette** below.

If not serving immediately, refrigerate the salad, but bring it to room temperature before serving.

1 cup quinoa

1½ cups water

⅓ cup pistachio nuts

2 stalks celery, sliced

3 scallions, green tops removed, sliced

¼ cup dried cranberries, coarsely chopped

 Quinoa is so versatile. You can eat it warm or cold, and it blends with many flavors. Try using it as substitute for any grain or pasta.

dijon mustard vinaigrette

Whisk together vinegar, Dijon mustard, sea salt, and black pepper in a small deep bowl. Slowly pour in the extra virgin olive oil into the bowl while whisking until dressing has emulsified.

2 tablespoons white wine vinegar

1 tablespoon Dijon mustard

¼ teaspoon sea salt

Black pepper

¼ cup extra virgin olive oil

macho salad

Serves 4

2 boneless, skinless chicken breasts, cut into cubes

1 tablespoon herbes de Provence

1 tablespoon extra virgin olive oil

2 heads romaine lettuce, chopped

½ head red cabbage, chopped

2 avocados, chopped

1 cup trail mix (dried cranberries, pistachios, almonds)

½ cup pitted dates, chopped

Season chicken with herbes de Provence and sauté in olive oil. Remove chicken from pan and set aside.

Sauté red cabbage in olive oil in the same pan you cooked the chicken, and set aside.

Mix all ingredients together in a large bowl and top with **Citrus Vinaigrette** below.

tip▶ This salad is a perfect combination of savory and sweet. It is a salad full of strong characteristics and flavors, making it "macho".

citrus vinaigrette

½ cup red wine vinegar

½ orange, juiced

⅓ cup extra virgin olive oil

½ tablespoon honey

Sea salt to taste

Combine dressing ingredients in a food processor and mix well.

kale caesar salad

Serves 4

Chop kale into small pieces and add to a large salad bowl.

In a small skillet over medium-low heat, brown breadcrumbs with 1 tablespoon extra virgin olive oil until crispy.

Drizzle **Caesar Dressing** below onto kale and massage into the salad. Your hands actually work best. The more you handle and stir the kale the softer it will be and the dressing will absorb into the leaves.

Top kale salad with bread crumbs and parmesan cheese.

1 large bunch kale, spines removed, rinsed and dried

¼ cup Italian seasoned panko breadcrumbs (see tip)

¼ cup parmesan cheese, shredded

tip▶ May use hemp seeds in place of breadcrumbs but do not heat. Massaging the dressing into the kale leaves will help to break down the texture of the kale so it is easier to eat.

caesar dressing

Mix olive oil, Dijon, lemon, garlic, sea salt and black pepper in a small food processor until well blended.

¼ cup extra virgin olive oil

1 tablespoon Dijon mustard

1 lemon, juiced

10 cloves garlic, minced

Sea salt & black pepper to taste

 Caesar dressing is not usually made with the healthiest ingredients. Using Dijon mustard and lots of garlic is a healthy way to mimic that delicious Caesar flavor.

beet salad

Served 2-4

3 medium beets, peeled and sliced

½ cucumber, peeled and sliced

4 bibb lettuce leaves or a bunch of baby spinach

1 pound block feta cheese, thinly sliced

matt: *This beet salad makes non-beet lovers think twice.*

Make **Horseradish Sauce** below and put in refrigerator for 30 minutes.

Preheat oven to 350°F.

Spread beet slices on a cookie sheet in a single layer and bake for 15 minutes. Turn and cook another 15 minutes.

Place one lettuce leaf or one layer of spinach leaves on each of 4 salad plates.

Layer beets, cucumber, and feta cheese on top of spinach or lettuce, and then repeat the layers.

Top with a couple tablespoons of Horseradish Sauce below.

horseradish sauce

1 cup plain fat free Greek yogurt

2 tablespoons extra virgin olive oil

1 tablespoon prepared horseradish

Sea salt & black pepper to taste

Whisk together yogurt, horseradish, olive oil, sea salt, and black pepper together and put in refrigerator for 30 minutes.

 Greek yogurt is thicker and creamier than regular yogurt since most of the whey has been removed. Plus, it contains twice the protein of regular yogurt and less lactose as well. It also serves as a healthy substitute for mayonnaise and sour cream.

broccoli salad

Serves 4-6

1 head broccoli, chopped into small bite-sized pieces

1 cup whole almonds, toasted and coarsely chopped

¼ cup raisins

½ medium red onion, finely chopped

4 strips bacon or turkey bacon, cooked and chopped

Toss the broccoli with toasted almonds, raisins, red onion, and bacon.

Pour the **Ranch Dressing** below over the salad, and toss well.

Season with additional sea salt and black pepper to taste.

 Look for organic bacon that does not contain nitrates. Nitrates are preservatives added to bacon and cured meats to preserve color and increase shelf life.

ranch dressing/dip

¾ cup unsweetened almond milk

1 cup nonfat plain Greek yogurt

2 teaspoons onion powder

1 teaspoon garlic powder

1 tablespoon fresh dill

1 tablespoon fresh chives or diced green onions

Sea salt & black pepper to taste

Whisk all ingredients together until creamy. Refrigerate in airtight container for up to 7 days. It will thicken after refrigeration.

goddess salad

Serves 2

Heat a medium skillet over medium heat. Add in pecans and cook for 5 to 10 minutes or until toasted. Turn off heat and drizzle pecans with agave nectar. Let sit for 10 minutes.

Combine all salad ingredients and toss to mix.

Toss salad with **Dijon Mustard Vinaigrette** below and mix well.

tip▶ Serve with grilled chicken or salmon.

¼ cup pecans

1 tablespoon agave nectar or honey

2 hearts romaine lettuce, washed and chopped

½ cup hearts of palm, drained and chopped

¼ cup dried cherries

¼ cup red onion, chopped

½ cup cherry tomatoes, halved

dijon mustard vinaigrette

Whisk together vinegar, Dijon mustard, sea salt, and black pepper in a small deep bowl. Slowly pour in the extra virgin olive oil into the bowl while whisking until dressing has emulsified.

2 tablespoons white wine vinegar

1 tablespoon Dijon mustard

¼ teaspoon sea salt

Black pepper

¼ cup extra virgin olive oil

thai peanut salad

Serves 6

Prepare **Soy Awesome Dressing** below and let sit in refrigerator 10-30 minutes.

Wash and chop the cabbage, green onions, cucumber, and carrots, and place in large salad bowl.

Leave some green onions to top the salad

Use a small fry pan to warm the raw peanuts (3-5 minutes); be careful not to burn them.

Dress the salad with as much dressing as you desire. Save any unused dressing fur future use.

Top the salad with the roasted peanuts and sprinkle on the reserved green onion.

1 bunch napa cabbage

1 bunch green onions

1 cup carrots, shredded

1 cucumber, diced

½ cup pan roasted peanuts

matt: *I came up with this recipe after visiting Paris of all places. I stumbled upon a food truck down by the Seine River and ordered a Thai Peanut Salad. Since I loved everything about this salad, I created this recipe in tribute.*

soy awesome dressing

Whisk all ingredients together in a small mixing bowl.

Let sit for 10-30 minutes in refrigerator.

1 tablespoon rice vinegar

½ cup extra virgin olive oil

1 tablespoon toasted sesame oil

2 teaspoons Braggs Liquid Aminos or soy sauce

1 teaspoon garlic, minced

Sea salt & black pepper

Choose organic or "Certified Non-GMO" when using soy and soy sauce products. Bragg's Liquid Aminos is a healthier non-GMO alternative to soy sauce and contains less sodium.

black bean mango salad

Serves 6

¼ cup extra virgin olive oil

¼ cup balsamic vinegar

Juice of 1 lime

2 15-ounce cans black beans, rinsed and drained (see note)

1 15-ounce can whole kernel corn, drained

1 green bell pepper, chopped

1 red pepper, chopped

½ cup green onions, chopped

2 avocados, cubed

2 mangos, peeled and chopped

Sea salt & black pepper to taste

Mix olive oil, vinegar, and lime juice in the bottom of a large mixing bowl.

Add remaining ingredients and toss to coat with dressing.

Refrigerate 1 hour before serving.

Serve as a salad or dip with organic blue corn tortilla chips.

tip ▶ Can be made in advance. Leave out avocado until ready to serve.

 Rinsing and draining beans can reduce the sodium content by 40%.

lentil & black bean salad

Serves 4-6

Put lentils into a small sauce pan with plenty of water to cover. Bring to a slow simmer and cook until lentils are tender, about 40-60 minutes for green lentils or 30-40 minutes for brown ones. Drain lentils and let cool slightly.

While lentils are cooling, rinse and drain the black beans and then dry with paper towel.

Mix chicken stock, Dijon mustard, lime juice, Worcestershire sauce, and garlic together in a small bowl.

Grind together cumin seed, chili powder, herb seasoning salt, and black pepper and add to bowl with chicken stock mixture.

Slowly drizzle olive oil into the stock mixture while whisking vigorously. Add hot sauce to taste.

When lentils are slightly cooled, add the black beans and half of the dressing and let marinate while you prep the rest of the ingredients.

Add the red pepper and green onions to lentil and bean mixture.

Stir in the rest of the dressing and add the chopped cilantro.

Salad is best if refrigerated for an hour before serving but can be served immediately.

1 cup (about ½ pound) lentils, rinsed and drained

1 can black beans, rinsed and drained

2 tablespoons chicken stock

1 teaspoon Dijon mustard

1 tablespoon fresh lime juice (can use apple cider vinegar)

1 teaspoon Worcestershire sauce

1 teaspoon garlic, finely minced

1 teaspoon cumin

½ teaspoon ancho chili powder (or any mild chili powder)

½ teaspoon of your favorite herb seasoning mix

Black pepper to taste

2 tablespoons extra virgin olive oil

Hot sauce to taste

1 cup red bell pepper, finely chopped

½ cup green onion (scallions) green part only, finely chopped

1 cup fresh cilantro, finely chopped

basil parmesan tuna salad

Serves 4 (Pictured at right)

Mix together and let sit in refrigerator for 1 hour before serving.

2 5-ounce cans tongol tuna in water

1 tablespoon parmesan cheese, grated

½ cup red pepper, chopped small

½ green onion, chopped

Sea salt & black pepper to taste

5 fresh basil leaves, chopped

1-2 tablespoons extra virgin olive oil

Juice of ½ lemon

> Tongol tuna contains lower mercury levels than other tunas and is produced using responsible fishing practices. Most of all, tongol tuna has a much fresher taste than other canned tunas.

fresh & light tuna salad

Serves 4

Mix together tuna, carrots, celery, and onion.

Whisk together the remaining ingredients and toss on tuna mixture.

2 cans tongol tuna

1 carrot, finely diced

1 stalk celery, finely diced

½ small red onion, finely diced

1 cup extra virgin olive oil

½ cup orange or lemon juice

¼ tablespoon lemon or orange zest

½ teaspoon sea salt

1 tablespoon honey

¼ cup chopped basil

1½ teaspoons white wine vinegar

tip▶ You can make this in advance and pack it for a quick lunch on the ski slopes, a camping trip, or picnic.

awesome chicken salad

Serves 6

Whisk together mayonnaise, lemon juice, curry powder, and salt and black pepper. Store in the refrigerator 1 hour before mixing with remaining ingredients.

Mix all ingredients in a large bowl and combine with the dressing.

For the dressing:

⅔ cup olive oil mayonnaise

Juice of ½ lemon

2 tablespoons curry powder (more or less to taste)

Sea salt & black pepper to taste

For the salad:

4 boneless, skinless chicken breasts (poached in broth), cooled and chopped

½ cup black or wild rice (cooked and cooled)

1 cup celery, chopped

4 scallions, chopped

1 cup walnuts chopped

¾ cup dried cranberries or cherries

tip ▶ This can be served wrapped in large lettuce leaves or collard greens.

entrées

herb roasted chicken

Serves 4-6 (pictured on page 110)

1 3-4 pound whole organic chicken

4 sprigs fresh thyme or rosemary

1 lemon, quartered

1 onion, quartered

Extra virgin olive oil

Sea salt & black pepper

Preheat oven to 350°F.

Wash and dry the chicken.

Place it in a 13x9 inch roasting pan.

Gently separate the skin from the breast of the chicken to slide in one sprig of fresh thyme or rosemary on each breast.

Rub a light layer of extra virgin olive oil over entire chicken and season with salt and black pepper. Don't forget to oil and season the back side of the chicken.

Place a sprig of fresh herbs under the bird and on top.

Insert the quartered lemon and onion into the chicken cavity.

Fold the wings under the chicken, and tie the legs together.

Roast the chicken for approximately 1.5 hours until internal temperature of the thickest part of the leg reaches 160°F.

Baste occasionally with the pan drippings. Let sit for 20 minutes before carving.

Enjoy.

turmeric & sesame grilled chicken

Serves 4

Rinse chicken and pat dry.

Drizzle chicken with olive oil, and season with sea salt, black pepper, turmeric, and sesame seeds. Turn and season again on the second side.

Preheat a grill pan on medium-high.

Place the chicken on the grill pan and do not touch until the chicken is sufficiently browned. Turn chicken over and brown sufficiently on the second side.

8 boneless, skinless chicken thighs or 4 boneless, skinless chicken breasts

1 tablespoon extra virgin olive oil

Sea salt & black pepper

1 tablespoon ground turmeric

1 tablespoon sesame seeds

 Turmeric is one of the most powerful antioxidant-rich herbs used to help with pain, inflammation, brain health, digestion, and immune function.

go-to marinade

½ cup red wine vinegar

½ cup Bragg's Liquid Aminos

1 cup organic ketchup

¼ cup extra virgin olive oil

2 cloves garlic, chopped

Whisk all ingredients in a small mixing bowl.

Brush on chicken, steak, or fish, or use as a marinade for steak and chicken kabobs.

 On those nights when you need a quick chicken, steak, or fish preparation, use a bottle of salad dressing for an easy marinade. Look for salad dressings that use extra virgin olive oil or expeller pressed oils. These oils provide the most flavor and nutrition.

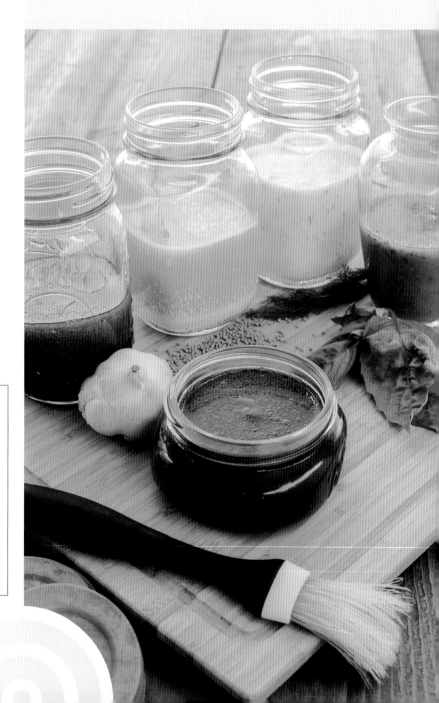

basic breaded chicken

Serves 4

Slice chicken in half lengthwise if thick. Place on a cutting board and place a sheet of saran wrap over chicken. Pound chicken with a meat mallet until flat.

Remove saran wrap and season chicken with sea salt and black pepper or favorite seasoning.

Combine egg and almond milk in a shallow bowl. Place coconut flour or breading of choice in another shallow bowl. Dip chicken in egg mixture then dry mixture, shaking off excess.

Heat a skillet with 2 tablespoons extra virgin olive oil over medium high heat. Place a single layer of the breaded chicken in the hot skillet flipping once until brown and crispy on both sides (about 4-5 minutes per side). Repeat with remaining chicken if necessary.

Place browned chicken on baking sheet and bake at 350°F for 10 minutes to ensure the chicken is cooked through and to keep warm.

1 pound boneless, skinless chicken breasts

Sea salt, black pepper, and/or favorite seasoning

1 egg

2 tablespoons unsweetened almond milk

2 cups breading (coconut flour, ground nuts, breadcrumbs, or panko)

tip▶ For nights when you simply don't know what to make for dinner—"pound it, bread it, fry it, eat it!"

 If using breadcrumbs, use an organic version if available.

easy cookie sheet dinner

Serves 1-12

Scale to serve more.

Preheat oven to 425°F.

Lightly coat cookie sheet with olive oil.

Place potato slices on cookie sheet in a single layer; sprinkle with 1 teaspoon of extra virgin olive oil. Place cookie sheet on bottom rack in oven and roast for 10 minutes.

Remove the tray from the oven and carefully turn the potatoes.

Season the chicken breast with lemon pepper and place on the cookie sheet along with the vegetables. Roast for an additional 10 minutes.

Turn the chicken and toss the potatoes and vegetables to keep them from getting too browned.

Dinner is done when vegetables are tender and chicken is cooked through.

Season with sea salt and black pepper to taste.

1 large sweet potato or baking potato, peeled and cut into ½-inch slices or cubes

3 teaspoons extra virgin olive oil, divided

8 ounces boneless, skinless chicken breast

½ teaspoon lemon pepper

8 ounces cleaned asparagus, green beans, onions, mushrooms, broccoli, and/or any other preferred vegetables

tip▶ This cookie sheet dinner is a great recipe for a quick weeknight meal.

family famous chicken & noodles

Serves 4

1 package boneless, skinless chicken thighs (about 6-8 pieces)

1 cup flour (as an alternate, use half almond flour and half unbleached white flour)

¼ cup parsley, chopped (reserve some for garnish)

2 eggs

2 tablespoons extra virgin olive oil

2 cups chicken broth

1 pint mushrooms, sliced

1 box whole grain pasta of choice

2 tablespoons parsley, chopped

Rinse and dry chicken. Season generously with sea salt and black pepper.

Place flour and parsley in a shallow bowl. In another shallow bowl whisk eggs.

Dip chicken into egg mixture and then in flour mixture until coated.

Heat extra virgin olive oil in a large deep fry pan over medium-high heat.

Brown chicken in olive oil 5-7 minutes per side.

Add the sliced mushrooms and chicken broth to the chicken in the pan.

Simmer over medium heat until broth thickens, about 10-12 minutes.

Meanwhile, cook pasta according to package directions.

Serve chicken and sauce over cooked pasta.

Sprinkle with fresh parsley.

kristen & matt:
We request "Chicken & Noodles" for our birthday dinner every year!

chicken satay

Serves 4

Slice the chicken thinly and arrange in a deep dish.

Mix the Bragg's, lime juice, and olive oil together well. Pour over chicken and let marinate in fridge overnight or for at least 1 hour.

Remove the chicken from the marinade and thread onto skewers.

Cook on the grill on medium-high heat until cooked through.

Meanwhile, prepare the peanut sauce by combining all ingredients. Whisk vigorously until a smooth consistency. Add more water for a thinner consistency.

Serve chicken with satay sauce.

For the chicken and marinade:

1 pound boneless, skinless chicken breasts

4 tablespoons Bragg's Liquid Aminos

1 tablespoon extra virgin olive oil

¼ cup fresh lime juice

For the peanut sauce:

¼ cup natural peanut butter

⅓ cup warm water

1 tablespoon Bragg's Liquid Aminos

1 tablespoon apple cider vinegar

1 teaspoon honey

1 teaspoon fresh ginger

tip ▶ Peanut Sauce is delicious with chicken, steak, veggies, and rice.

hawaiian grilled chicken

Serves 6

For the chicken and marinade:

2 pounds boneless, skinless chicken thighs

½ cup Bragg's or Coconut Liquid Aminos

1 13.5-ounce can coconut milk

1 teaspoon sesame oil

1 bunch green onions, chopped (save some for the top for garnish)

½ teaspoon minced garlic

For the rice:

1 cup multi-color whole grain brown rice

4 cups vegetable broth

1 tablespoon extra virgin olive oil

½ white onion, chopped

4 stalks of celery, diced

4 large carrots, diced

Combine all of the listed chicken ingredients in a resealable plastic bag. Marinate chicken for at least 4 hours or overnight.

Bring rice, broth, and oil to a boil. Add in onion, celery, and carrots, and cook as long as the rice package directions indicate. Fluff with a fork. Season with additional sea salt and black pepper or Bragg's if desired.

While the rice is cooking, grill chicken at medium-low heat for 5-7 minutes per side or until cooked through.

Serve the chicken with rice and top with green onions.

Bragg's Liquid Aminos is a Certified Non-GMO liquid protein concentrate, derived from soybeans. Coconut Liquid Aminos is also a healthy substitute for soy sauce and is made from coconut tree sap that has been combined with sea salt.

slow cooker asian cashew chicken

Serves 4-6

Combine all ingredients except cashews in a large slow cooker. Cook on high for 4 hours or on low for 8 hours or until chicken is tender.

Turn slow cooker off and let sit for 30 minutes, then pull the chicken into shreds using two forks.

Serve chicken over whole grain rice and top with cashews and a side of sautéed spinach.

¼ cup Bragg's Liquid Aminos

2 tablespoons rice vinegar

2 tablespoons organic ketchup

1 tablespoon coconut sugar

1 garlic clove, minced

1 tablespoon ginger, grated

1 package boneless, skinless chicken thighs or breasts

½ cup raw cashews

 Coconut sugar is made by boiling and dehydrating the sap of the coconut palm. It contains more nutrients and is lower on the glycemic index than table sugar

slow cooker chicken nachos

Serves 6-8

Place chicken, tomatoes with juice, chilies with juice, and taco seasoning into a slow cooker. Cook on low for 8 hours or high for 4 hours.

One half hour before serving, pull out the chicken and shred. Add chicken back into slow cooker.

Add in the beans, onions, corn and its juice if needed, and cheese. Cook for another 30 minutes on high.

Serve over tortilla chips.

2 boneless, skinless chicken breasts

1 14.5-ounce can diced tomatoes and can juice

1 4-ounce can green chilies, chopped, retain and use the juice

1 package taco seasoning (see page 83 for homemade Taco Seasoning recipe)

1 14.5-ounce can refried beans

¾ cup onion, chopped

1 14.5-ounce can sweet corn, and juice if needed

5 ounces shredded cheddar cheese

Garnish with sliced avocado or guacamole (see Guaca-Money recipe page 56) and serve with 1 bag tortilla chips

chicken parmesan minus the pasta & parm

Serves 2

1 spaghetti squash

½ cup bread crumbs

1 teaspoon garlic powder

1 teaspoon sea salt

1 teaspoon black pepper

1 teaspoon onion powder

1 teaspoon rosemary

2 egg whites, whisked

2 boneless, skinless chicken breasts, pounded

2 tablespoons extra virgin olive oil

1 jar pasta sauce

Cut spaghetti squash in half and remove the seeds. Cook on a baking sheet with ½ inch of water for 60 minutes or until soft.

Mix all of the dry ingredients together. Dip the chicken in egg whites and then dry mixture.

In a large pan heat extra virgin olive oil and brown the chicken on both sides.

Once the chicken is brown, pour in the pasta sauce, cover and cook for 10-15 minutes until chicken is tender.

Serve chicken over the spaghetti squash.

 When using breadcrumbs, always choose an organic version to avoid hydrogenated oils and high fructose corn sugar.

bomb barbeque
pulled chicken

Serves 4

Place all ingredients in slow cooker and cook on low for 6-8 hours until meat is very tender.

Pull meat apart with a fork. Top with a sprinkle of smoked paprika.

kristen: *I first served this recipe at a house party for over 50 guests! It was a huge success and I will forever remember this day. When a small town girl makes a bomb barbeque sauce, it only seems right that it should be published.*

1 package boneless, skinless chicken thighs or breasts

1 cup organic ketchup

1 tablespoon brown sugar

1 tablespoon molasses

1 tablespoon red wine vinegar

¼ teaspoon cayenne pepper

½ tablespoon garlic powder

½ tablespoon dry mustard

½ tablespoon chili powder

½ teaspoon black pepper

½ teaspoon ground allspice

½ teaspoon ground cinnamon

1 onion, chopped

Sea salt to taste

Smoked paprika

lettuce wraps

Serves 4

Brown the ground chicken with 1 tablespoon olive oil in a large sauté pan over medium-high heat.

Add remaining 1 tablespoon olive oil to another medium pan and sauté the yellow onions, mushrooms, and water chestnuts until the mushrooms become tender.

Once the chicken is cooked thoroughly, add in the cooked mushrooms, onions, and water chestnuts mixture. Add the sesame teriyaki sauce and heat 2-3 minutes until combined

Place individual lettuce leaves on a serving plate. Spoon a generous amount of the meat mixture in each lettuce leaf. Sprinkle with diced green onion and toasted sesame.

Garnish the plate with sriracha or hot sauce for added heat (optional).

Goes well with brown rice on the side.

1 pound ground organic chicken

2 tablespoons extra virgin olive oil

¼ cup yellow onion, diced

1 package sliced mushrooms washed and diced

¼ cup water chestnuts, diced

2 tablespoons sesame teriyaki sauce

1 teaspoon toasted sesame seeds

½ cup green onion, sliced

1 bunch Boston lettuce, washed and separated

Garnish with sriracha or your favorite hot sauce

matt: *Lettuce wraps are very popular, but many people don't make them at home. I came up with this recipe by trying a bunch of lettuce wraps and deciding what flavors and textures I preferred. These are really, really good!*

sun dried tomato & wild mushroom pasta

Serves 4-6

In small food processor place all Pesto Sauce ingredients and pulse until combined. Set aside.

Pound chicken breast to ¾-inch thickness. Lightly season chicken with sea salt and black pepper, and grill. Once grilled, slice into strips and set aside.

In a medium sauce pan boil chicken broth and Marsala wine for about 5 minutes to reduce. Once reduced, add dried mushrooms and simmer for 1-2 minutes longer. Turn off heat and let steep for 10-15 minutes. Remove the mushrooms from the broth, reserving broth.

Pour 1 cup of boiled water over the sun dried tomatoes and let soak for 2 minutes. Remove the sun dried tomatoes from the water and discard water.

Cook the pasta in boiling, salted water until al dente.

Cut the larger reconstituted mushrooms into quarters and thinly slice the sun dried tomatoes.

Heat 1 tablespoon olive oil in a large, deep sided sauté pan. Add garlic and sliced fresh mushrooms until the mushrooms have lost all of their water.

Add the dried mushrooms, chicken, and sun dried tomatoes. Season with sea salt and black pepper.

Add ½ the pesto mixture and the cooked pasta along with half of the reserved mushroom broth. Simmer until the broth evaporates slightly.

Add the remaining pesto and top with crumbled feta or goat cheese.

tip▶ The extra pesto sauce can be stored in the refrigerator for 2 weeks.

For the pesto sauce:

2 tablespoons extra virgin olive oil

½ cup fresh basil, chopped

½ teaspoon black pepper

½ teaspoon sea salt

½ teaspoon fresh oregano

½ teaspoon fresh thyme

¼ teaspoon red pepper flakes

2 boneless, skinless chicken breasts

2 cups chicken broth

1 tablespoon Marsala wine

1 cup dried wild mushrooms (morals and northern wild)

10-12 sun dried tomatoes, dried no oil

2 cups whole wheat gemelli pasta

2 tablespoons extra virgin olive oil

1 clove garlic, chopped

1½ cups fresh mushrooms, thinly sliced

2-3 tablespoons feta cheese

bison umami burger

Serves 4

For the burgers:

1 pound ground bison

½ onion, chopped

1 tablespoon Worcestershire sauce

½ teaspoon sea salt

¼ teaspoon black pepper or 1 teaspoon steak seasoning

For the umami tapenade:

3-4 portabella mushrooms (2 cups), cut into finely diced pieces

1 tablespoon black truffle oil

Sea salt & black pepper

Additional ingredients/ toppings:

Fresh basil

Buffalo mozzarella, sliced

Tomato, sliced

Extra virgin olive oil mayonnaise

Hamburger buns

To make tapenade, heat a skillet over medium-high heat and add in mushrooms. Cover and let cook until tender, about 10 minutes. Remove pan from heat and drizzle with truffle oil. Stir to mix and reserve for later.

Preheat grill to medium-high heat.

Combine burger ingredients in a large bowl and use hands to mix. Form into 3-4 patties (depending on desired size).

Drizzle burgers with a little extra virgin olive oil to prevent from sticking and place on grill. Cook for 3-4 minutes then flip.

After 1 minute on second side, top burgers with a piece of basil and mozzarella. Continue to cook until cheese is melted, about 2 minutes. Remove from grill and let sit.

To assemble burgers, add umami tapenade to bottom of bun, and top with bison burger, tomato and a little mayo. Enjoy!

 Umami is a Japanese word that describes a meaty or savory taste. Tomatoes and mushrooms are high in free form glutamate which provides a natural umami flavor. Black truffles are a rare and extravagant mushroom with an intense meaty flavor.

marinated flank steak

Serves 4

Mix marinade ingredients together in a large resealable plastic bag and add flank steak.

Let sit in the refrigerator overnight or for at least 4 hours.

Remove steak from refrigerator at least 20-30 minutes before grilling. To grill, remove steak from marinade and discard the marinade. Grill 5 minutes per side for medium rare.

Let steak rest at least 15 minutes before carving. To serve, cut steak diagonally across the grain into thin slices.

1.5 to 2 pound flank steak

Marinade:

½ cup extra virgin olive oil

⅓ cup Bragg's Liquid Aminos

¼ cup red wine vinegar

½ lemon, juiced

1 tablespoon Worcestershire sauce

1 teaspoon dry mustard

1 clove garlic, minced

¼ teaspoon black pepper

matt: *This marinated flank steak has been the center of many special occasions at our house.*

1-2 cups basmati rice

For the tzatziki sauce:

1 large English cucumber, shredded with cheese grater

5 mint leaves, chopped

2 cups Greek yogurt

1 large clove garlic, minced

½ cup golden raisins

For the curry sauce:

1 tablespoon ground cumin

1 teaspoon ground cinnamon

¼ teaspoon ground cloves

2 teaspoons black pepper

1 teaspoon ground turmeric

2 teaspoons paprika

¼ teaspoon cayenne

4-6 garlic cloves, chopped

1 teaspoon ginger root, peeled and chopped

½ cup apple cider vinegar

2 tablespoons fresh parsley, chopped

For the meat:

2 tablespoons extra virgin olive oil

½ large red onion, sliced

1 serrano pepper, sliced down the center, seeds removed

2 pounds beef sirloin, cut into ½-inch cubes

1 teaspoon sea salt

beef curry

Serves 4-6

Cook basmati rice according to package directions.

For tzatziki sauce:

Combine all ingredients in a small bowl and refrigerate for 20-30 minutes.

To prepare the curry sauce:

Combine the cumin, cinnamon, cloves, black pepper, turmeric, paprika, and cayenne in a mini food processor. Add the garlic, ginger, and apple cider vinegar, and mix until combined. Set aside.

To assemble:

Cook onions in Dutch oven over medium heat until tender. Add the sliced serrano peppers and sauté for an additional 12 minutes. Keep stirring, don't let the onions burn.

Add the curry sauce to the onion and peppers, and continue stirring for about 2 minutes or until the mixture thickens and the moisture has evaporated. Add 1 cup warm water to the food processor and mix to take up the remaining spices.

Add the cubed meet to the onion and pepper mixture. Stir occasionally for 5 minutes while the meat cooks and gathers the curry sauce. Add sea salt to taste.

Add the water from the processor to the beef mixture. Bring to a boil, then lower the heat to simmer for 30 minutes. Add the chopped parsley and remove from heat.

Serve over basmati rice and top with the tzatziki sauce.

matt: This is a great recipe to start with if you have never cooked with curry. My wife Holly and I stumbled upon an Indian restaurant on a side street in Old Town Nice, France. That visit inspired this recipe.

sweet potato shepherd's pie

Serves 6

3 large sweet potatoes

1 tablespoon extra virgin olive oil

1 large onion, diced

1 green bell pepper, diced

3 cloves garlic, minced

1 pound ground bison

1 package taco seasoning (or use Taco Seasoning recipe on page 83)

1 14.5 ounce can diced tomatoes

2 cups shredded cheddar cheese, divided

½ cup original coconut milk

Preheat oven to 375°F.

Place sweet potatoes on a baking sheet lined with aluminum foil and bake for 90 minutes or until sweet potatoes are tender. Remove sweet potatoes and set aside to cool. Turn the oven up to 400°F.

Meanwhile, in a large skillet heat 1 tablespoon extra virgin olive oil over medium heat. Add the onion, pepper, and garlic. Season with sea salt and black pepper, and cook until tender, about 5-7 minutes. Remove vegetables to a plate and set aside.

Add bison to skillet and sprinkle with taco seasoning. Heat until cooked through and browned. Add in the cooked vegetables and canned tomatoes. Cook for 5 minutes or until mixture comes to a low boil.

Peel the cooled sweet potatoes and add to a large bowl. Blend slightly with a handheld mixer, and then add the coconut milk and continue to blend until the potato mixture is creamy. Stir in 1 cup of cheese.

Spray a large casserole dish with cooking spray. Spread bison mixture evenly on the bottom of casserole dish and sprinkle with the remaining cheese. Spoon the sweet potato mixture evenly over the top. Bake for 10 minutes and turn on low broil cooking for 10 minutes more or until slightly browned on top.

 Traditional Shepherd's Pie is usually made with mashed white potatoes. Using sweet potatoes instead is a tasty way to add more vitamin A, vitamin C, calcium, and iron.

tip ▶ Reach for this when you simply need a comfort food fix.

throwback meatloaf

Serves 4-6

Preheat oven to 350°F. Combine all ingredients in a large bowl and mix thoroughly.

Press into a 9 inch loaf pan.

Bake for 45-50 minutes or until internal temperature reaches 160°F. Spread ¼ cup tomato salsa or organic ketchup on meatloaf during last 15 minutes of baking.

Let stand 5 minutes before slicing.

tip ▶ For burgers, form into patties and broil, bake, or grill as desired.

1½ pounds ground bison or turkey

1 10-ounce package frozen chopped spinach, thawed and drained

2 egg whites

1½ teaspoons Italian seasoning

1 cup rolled oats

½ cup onions, chopped

½ cup carrots, shredded

1 small apple, shredded

⅓ cup almond or coconut milk

½ teaspoon sea salt

¼ teaspoon black pepper

¼ cup tomato salsa or organic ketchup

5 ingredient meatloaf

Serves 4

Preheat oven to 350°F.

Combine all ingredients and mix gently by hand.

Press into loaf pan and bake for 50 minutes, until cooked through.

1 pound ground turkey or bison

2 eggs

1 12-ounce can organic cream of mushroom soup

1 cup rolled oats

¾ cup onions, chopped

Sea salt & black pepper to taste

zucchini "noodle" lasagna

Serves 8-10

Brown meat in the olive oil. Add onion, celery, and garlic, and sauté for 5 minutes until translucent. Stir in tomatoes, broth, tomato paste, hot sauce, black pepper, thyme, basil, sea salt, and bay leaves. Bring to a boil; reduce heat, and simmer uncovered for 35 minutes, stirring occasionally. Stir in parsley and cook for another 2 minutes. Discard bay leaves and set sauce aside.

Place oven rack on the bottom. Preheat oven to 450°F.

Coat a large cookie sheet with extra virgin olive oil. To make zucchini "noodles," wash zucchini and cut ends off; cut lengthwise into ½-inch thick slices. Arrange zucchini slices on cookie sheet; sprinkle with ½ tablespoon olive oil and sprinkle with black pepper. Roast in oven for 10 minutes. Turn slices over and roast for an additional 5-10 minutes or until tender and nicely browned. Remove pan from oven and set aside.

Reduce oven temperature to 350°F.

Combine cottage cheese, ½ cup parmesan cheese, and egg white in a small bowl and set aside.

Brush a 9x13 inch glass baking dish with olive oil. Add a thin layer of sauce to cover the bottom. Layer half of the zucchini slices, half of the cottage cheese mixture, and half the shredded mozzarella. Spread half of the sauce over the layers, and then repeat starting with zucchini. Sprinkle 2 tablespoons parmesan cheese on top.

Bake uncovered for 20 minutes or until slightly browned and bubbly. Remove the dish from the oven and let it rest for 15 minutes before serving.

tip ▶ This can be frozen before baking for up to 1 month. Hard textured vegetables are great substitutes for white lasagna noodles.

For the sauce:

1 tablespoon extra virgin olive oil

2 pounds ground bison, turkey, or turkey Italian sausage

2 cups onions, chopped

1 cup celery, chopped

4 large cloves garlic, minced

2 14.5-ounce cans Italian stewed tomatoes

1 14.5-ounce can beef or chicken broth

1 6-ounce can tomato paste

Hot sauce to taste

½ teaspoon black pepper

½ teaspoon dried thyme

1 teaspoon dried sweet basil

⅛ teaspoon sea salt

2 bay leaves

¼ cup fresh Italian flat leaf parsley, chopped

For the lasagna:

1 pound (3 medium) zucchini

½ teaspoon black pepper

1 tablespoon extra virgin olive oil

1 cup low-fat cottage cheese or ricotta cheese

1 egg white, slightly beaten

½ cup plus 2 tablespoons parmesan cheese, grated

1 cup (4 ounces) part-skim mozzarella cheese, shredded

eggplant parmesan

Serves 4

1 medium eggplant, peeled and cut into 1-inch thick round slices

2 eggs, beaten slightly in a flat bowl

½ cup breadcrumbs

1 teaspoon sea salt

1 teaspoon black pepper

1 teaspoon garlic powder

1 teaspoon onion powder

½ cup parmesan cheese

2 cups tomato sauce or prepared spaghetti sauce (or use Lasagna Sauce on page 139)

Pre-heat oven to 350°F

Combine all dry ingredients (except for cheese) and spread evenly on a plate.

Dredge the eggplant in the egg and then the breadcrumb mixture.

Place the breaded eggplant in a single layer on a slightly oiled cookie sheet. Bake for 5 minutes on each side.

Broil the eggplant until it turns crispy and golden brown then turn and brown the other side. Once the eggplant is lightly browned on the second side, sprinkle with parmesan cheese and continue to broil until cheese is melted.

Pour heated tomato sauce over eggplant and serve.

 When you see recipes calling for breadcrumbs, flour, sauces, spices, etc., follow the Food Target and select the highest quality possible. Don't make this with the typical store-bought trans fat breadcrumbs. Make or buy real organic breadcrumbs.

coconut pumpkin alfredo sauce

Serves 4

1 14-ounce can coconut milk

1 14-ounce can pureéd pumpkin

Sea salt & black pepper to taste

1 teaspoon garlic powder

1 teaspoon onion powder

Garnish with chopped fresh chives

Combine all ingredients in a small saucepan and bring to a low simmer. Add to your favorite pasta, gnocchi, tortellini, or ravioli. Sprinkle with fresh chives.

cauliflower crust pizza

Serves 4

To prepare the crust:

Preheat the oven to 450°F.

Spray a cookie sheet or pizza stone with nonstick extra virgin olive oil spray (or use a nonstick surface).

Shred the cauliflower into small crumbles. You can use a food processor if you wish, but be careful not to over process. You want dry crumbles, not a purée. Pat dry if needed.

In a medium bowl, mix cauliflower crumbles with the remaining crust ingredients. Pat the "crust" into a 9-12 inch round on the prepared pan. Bake for 15 minutes (or until golden).

Remove the crust from the oven and turn the heat up to broil. If crust is still watery after 15 minutes, broil on high to get moisture out. Don't let it burn!

To assemble:

Spread the sauce on top of the baked crust, leaving a ½-inch border around the edge.

Sprinkle the mozzarella cheese on top of the sauce. Top with the sliced mushrooms and onions. Broil the pizza 3 to 4 minutes, or until the toppings are hot and the cheese is melted and bubbly.

Cut into 6 slices and serve immediately.

Crust:

1½ cups cauliflower, finely chopped (about ½ large head)

1 large egg

1 cup parmesan cheese, finely shredded

1 teaspoon dried oregano

½ teaspoon dried minced garlic (or fresh garlic)

½ teaspoon onion powder

½ teaspoon sea salt

Toppings:

½ cup pizza sauce or Lasagna Sauce (see recipe on page 139)

¼ cup mushrooms of choice, thinly sliced

¼ cup yellow onions, thinly sliced

½ cup block mozzarella, crumbled

indian style shrimp

Serves 2-3

Cook the basmati rice according to package directions. Five minutes before the rice is done, add the diced Roma tomatoes and chopped cilantro. Cover and finish cooking the rice.

Season the shrimp with curry, sea salt, black pepper, and cayenne pepper. Heat olive oil over medium heat in a shallow fry pan. Add the seasoned shrimp to the hot pan and cook for 2-3 minutes or until they turn pink.

Add the coconut milk to the shrimp and simmer for 3-5 minutes.

Taste the sauce and add seasoning as desired.

Serve over the rice.

1 cup basmati rice

2 Roma tomatoes, diced

1 tablespoon cilantro, chopped

1 pound raw shelled shrimp

1 tablespoon curry powder

Sea salt and black pepper to taste

1 teaspoon cayenne pepper (optional)

2 tablespoons extra virgin olive oil

1 cup condensed coconut milk

chilean sea bass with miso broth

Serves 2

½ cup white jasmine rice

1 cup chicken broth

½ cup water

2 tablespoons miso paste

1 tablespoon mushroom soup base or bouillon

1 teaspoon toasted sesame oil

1 teaspoon fresh ginger, minced

3 celery leaves

¼ cup chopped onion

2 4-ounce fillets Chilean sea bass

1 tablespoon extra virgin olive oil

2 green onions, chopped

Toasted sesame oil

Garnish with chopped green onions

Preheat oven to 375°F.

Cook rice according to package directions using water as the cooking liquid.

Meanwhile, combine chicken broth, water, miso, bouillon, sesame oil, ginger, celery leaves, and onion to a small saucepan. Cook over medium high heat for 15-20 minutes. Let sit for 5 minutes.

Season sea bass with salt and black pepper. Heat an oven proof skillet over medium-high heat. Add 1 tablespoon olive oil. Place sea bass skin side up in pan and cook for 5 minutes or until browned. Flip and cook 4 minutes more.

Place skillet in the oven and cook for 5 additional minutes or until fish flakes with a fork. (Depending on thickness you may not need to finish cooking in oven). Remove skin from sea bass before plating.

Add a heaping spoonful of rice to the center of a two bowls and top each with 1 fillet of sea bass.

Pour broth over sea bass and add a few drops of toasted sesame oil and a sprinkle of green onions.

baked mustard salmon

Serves 2

Preheat oven to 375°F.

Rinse and pat dry salmon. Sprinkle with sea salt and place skin side down in a baking dish.

Mix vinegar, mustards, and olive oil until well blended. Spoon over each fillet, covering completely.

Combine breadcrumbs with dried thyme, garlic powder, and sea salt. Press breadcrumbs onto fish. Bake until flaky, about 18 minutes.

8 ounces wild caught salmon fillet, skin on

1 tablespoon balsamic vinegar

¾ teaspoon dry mustard

1 tablespoon Dijon mustard

2 teaspoons extra virgin olive oil

¼ cup breadcrumbs

½ teaspoon dried thyme

¼ teaspoon garlic powder

½ teaspoon sea salt

 Choose wild-caught salmon vs. farm-raised. Wild-caught salmon contains more omega 3s and fewer PCBs than farm-raised salmon. Polychlorinated biphenyl or PCB is a toxic pollutant that has been found to contain cancer-causing chemicals according to the Environmental Working Group, EWG.

pesto crusted salmon

Serves 4

4 6-ounce salmon fillets

2 garlic cloves

1 cup broccoli florets

¼ cup extra virgin olive oil plus 2 tablespoons, separated

¼ parmesan cheese, grated

¼ cup unsalted shelled pistachios

Preheat the oven to 375°F.

Rub both sides of salmon fillets with 1 tablespoon olive oil.

Combine the rest of the ingredients and pulse in a food processor until mixture turns to a chunky purée. Season to taste with sea salt and black pepper. Coat the top of the salmon with the mixture.

Add 1 tablespoon extra virgin olive oil to a cast-iron skillet or non-stick pan over medium heat on the stovetop. Place salmon skin side down for 2-3 minutes until skin is sizzling.

Place the pan on the middle oven rack and bake for 8-10 minutes or until the salmon looks flaky and the pesto turns golden brown.

 The base of your typical pesto is basil. Use broccoli as your base instead to bump up the nutrition.

sides

easy acorn squash

Serves 4

1 acorn squash, halved and seeded

2 tablespoons virgin coconut oil

1 teaspoon sea salt

1-2 tablespoons pure maple syrup

Preheat oven to 350°F.

Place cut acorn squash face down on a baking sheet. Pour ½ inch water on the pan to create steam. Place in oven for 50 minutes or until the squash is soft enough to fork out of the skin.

Once it is cool enough to handle, scoop all the squash into a mixing bowl. Combine with the remaining ingredients and serve.

If you want to make this ahead of time, it will last 2 days in the refrigerator. Reheat in oven on 350°F.

maple glazed carrots & leeks

Serves 4

¼ cup virgin coconut oil, melted

1 tablespoon maple syrup

¼ teaspoon sea salt

¼ teaspoon cayenne pepper

6 medium carrots, peeled

3 large stalks of leeks, sliced

¼ cup parsley, chopped

Preheat oven to 375°F.

Combine virgin coconut oil, maple syrup, salt, and cayenne in a small bowl and whisk to mix.

Cut the carrots in half and slice lengthwise. Slice and clean leeks. Combine carrots and leeks on a baking sheet. Cover with virgin coconut oil mixture and toss to coat.

Place baking sheet in oven and cook for 20-25 minutes or until tender. Remove from oven and top with parsley before serving.

tip ▶ To clean leeks, cut off and discard the dark green leaves an inch or so above the white part. Slice white part; rinse in a colander under cold water.

roasted brussels sprouts

Serves 4

Preheat the oven to 375°F.

Cut off the stem end of the Brussels sprouts and cut in half. Place the halved sprouts in a bowl and combine all the ingredients.

Place the sprouts on a cooking sheet and bake for 40-50 minutes. They should be golden brown and slightly crispy.

tip▶ Any vegetable can be roasted in the oven. Try broccoli, cauliflower, or asparagus. Easy and delicious!

1½ pounds Brussels sprouts

2 tablespoons extra virgin olive oil

½ teaspoon sea salt

¼ teaspoon black pepper

2 garlic cloves, diced

Drizzle balsamic vinegar (optional)

153

roasted root vegetables

2 parsnips, cut into 1-inch pieces

2 large carrots, sliced

1 large sweet potato, cut into 1-inch pieces

2 purple potatoes, cut into 1-inch pieces

2 large yellow potatoes, cut into 1-inch pieces

2 tablespoons extra virgin olive oil

Sea salt & black pepper

1 tablespoon dried thyme

Preheat oven to 375°F.

Place all of the chopped vegetables on a large baking sheet.

Toss vegetables with olive oil, salt, and black pepper, and thyme.

Bake in oven for 30-45 minutes.

oven roasted beets

Serves 4

4 large or 8 small beets, peeled and sliced into circles

2 tablespoons extra virgin olive oil

Sea salt & black pepper

Preheat oven to 375°F.

Spread 1 tablespoon of olive oil on a large baking sheet.

Arrange beet slices on oiled baking sheet in a single layer.

Drizzle remaining 1 tablespoon olive oil on beet slices.

Season with sea salt and black pepper.

Bake in oven for 30 minutes until slightly crispy around the edges.

sweet potato tart

Serves 4-6

For the crust:

¾ cup walnuts

1¼ cups whole wheat pastry flour, plus more for dusting

1¼ cups quinoa or almond flour

2 tablespoons fresh thyme or rosemary, chopped

¾ teaspoon sea salt

¾ teaspoon black pepper

¼ cup extra virgin olive oil

¼ cup virgin coconut oil

7 tablespoons ice cold water

For the filling:

1½ pounds sweet potato, peeled and sliced

2 tablespoons extra virgin olive oil

½ teaspoon sea salt

¼ cup red or sweet onions, sliced and separated into rings

1 cup shredded cheddar cheese

1 large egg white mixed with 1 teaspoon water

1 teaspoon chopped fresh thyme or rosemary depending on what you chose for the crust

Preheat oven to 425°F.

To make the crust:

Prepare crust by placing walnuts in a food processor and pulse until finely ground. Add flours, thyme, sea salt, and black pepper, and pulse to combine. Add the solid virgin coconut oil and pulse until crumbly. Drizzle olive oil and ice water until mixture is combined. The dough will seem wetter than usual. Wrap the dough in plastic wrap and store in refrigerator for 15 minutes or up to 2 days.

To make the filling:

Toss the sweet potatoes with 1 tablespoon of olive oil, and season with sea salt and black pepper. Spread on two-thirds of a large cookie sheet. Toss the onions with 1 teaspoon of olive oil and season with sea salt and black pepper. Spread on remaining one-third of the cookie sheet. Roast in the oven for 10 minutes. Remove from the oven to cool slightly. Reduce oven temperature to 375°F.

Place dough on a floured nonstick baking mat or parchment paper. Dust the top of the dough with flour and roll into a 15-inch circle. Place the dough on the baking mat or parchment on a cookie sheet.

Sprinkle cheese on the crust, leaving a 2-inch border.

Place the sweet potatoes in two overlapping rings over the outside edge of the cheese.

Place the onions in a ring just inside those two sweet potatoes rows. Use remaining sweet potatoes to fill in an overlapping ring in the center.

Pick up the edges of the crust to form small pleats. Brush with the egg whites. Drizzle olive oil over the top of the tart and sprinkle with remaining thyme or rosemary.

Bake the tart for 50 minutes until lightly browned. Cool for 15 minutes before slicing.

oven fries

Serves 4

1 pound potatoes of choice, scrubbed clean, dried and cut into fries

1½ tablespoons extra virgin olive oil

Sea salt & black pepper to taste

Adjust oven rack to middle position and heat oven to 425°F.

Toss potatoes and olive oil on cookie sheet. Season with sea salt and black pepper and toss again to blend.

Spread potatoes out into a single layer.

Cook for 15 minutes; turn using metal spatula.

Return pan to oven and cook 10-15 minutes more until the potatoes begin to brown and get crunchy.

tip ▶ These fries can be made with red skin potatoes, sweet potatoes, or even root vegetables.

broccoli mashed potatoes

5 cups redskin potatoes, skins on and quartered

1 tablespoon virgin coconut oil

½ cup broccoli tops, chopped

1 teaspoon garlic powder

1 teaspoon onion powder

½ tablespoon sea salt

½ teaspoon black pepper

¼ cup almond milk

1 teaspoon prepared horseradish (optional)

Place potatoes in a large stainless steel pot (so you can mash the potatoes in the same pot). Add water to 2 inches above potatoes.

Boil until potatoes are fork tender, about 15 minutes.

Strain the potatoes and return to the same pot, but not to the heat.

While potatoes are still very hot, add in the coconut oil, broccoli tops, and all of the dried seasonings.

Blend with a hand mixer until most of the lumps are removed.

Add in the almond milk and horseradish. Beat until smooth and creamy.

tip ▶ Sprinkle with paprika to make it fancy.

mashed cauliflower

Serves 4 (pictured on page 111)

Place cauliflower and broth in a large pot. Cover partially with lid, allowing steam to escape.

Cook on medium heat until cauliflower is soft.

Mash with a potato masher, then mix in parmesan cheese and season with sea salt and black pepper.

1 large head cauliflower, chopped into florets

1 cup chicken or vegetable broth

Sea salt & black pepper to taste

Freshly grated parmesan cheese

 Mashed cauliflower has the same creamy texture as mashed potatoes but is much lower in calories which means you can go for seconds and not feel guilty! This cruciferous vegetable also contains fiber, vitamins, and minerals.

spaghetti squash

Serves 4

1 large spaghetti squash

1 jar organic marinara sauce or Lasagna Sauce, page 139

Preheat oven to 400°F.

Cut spaghetti squash in half, lengthwise. Scoop out seeds and place cut side down on a baking sheet.

Fill baking pan with 1 inch of water. Cook for 1 hour or until squash is soft. Refill water if necessary during cooking. Remove squash from oven and cool for 10 minutes.

Use a fork to scrape out squash to create "spaghetti."

Serve with your favorite pasta sauce or toppings.

 You can eat spaghetti squash the same way you eat spaghetti by simply twirling your fork around the strands. Since it is just one simple ingredient, it makes for a healthier alternative to white pasta. It is also naturally gluten-free and loaded with disease-fighting antioxidants.

zucchini "spaghetti"

Serves 4

Make zucchini spaghetti using a spiral slicer. Let sit in a strainer for about 30 minutes to drain.

For vegetarian sauce:

Sauté onion, black pepper, and garlic in 1 tablespoon olive oil until vegetables are tender. Pour in marinara sauce or Lasagna Sauce (see recipe page 139). Heat for 10 minutes.

For meat sauce:

Brown ground meat in 1 tablespoon olive oil. Add onion, pepper, and garlic, and sauté until vegetables are tender. Pour in marinara sauce or Lasagna Sauce (see recipe, page 139). Heat for 10 minutes.

Heat remaining 1 tablespoon olive oil in a large frying pan. Add the zucchini the pan and saute until heated through, about 5 minutes.

Pile zucchini on plate and top with sauce. Sprinkle with chopped basil.

For vegetarian option:

4 medium zucchini, ends removed

2 tablespoon extra virgin olive oil

1 jar organic marinara sauce or Lasagna Sauce page 139

1 tablespoon fresh basil, chopped

For meat option:

4 medium zucchini, ends removed

2 tablespoon extra virgin olive oil

1 pound ground beef, bison or turkey (optional)

1 medium onion, chopped

1 green pepper, chopped

1 clove garlic, chopped

1 jar organic marinara sauce or Lasagna Sauce page 139

1 tablespoon fresh basil, chopped

tip ▶ We use a spiral slicer to prepare the zucchini.

zucchini & squash casserole

Serves 6

2 medium zucchini or summer squash, sliced (can use a combination)

1 large onion, sliced and pulled into individual rings

2 large tomatoes, peeled and sliced

½ cup parmesan cheese, grated

Sea salt & black pepper to taste

Preheat oven to 400°F.

Grease a large, deep casserole dish with extra virgin olive oil.

In order, evenly layer half of the zucchini, onion, tomato, and cheese into casserole dish.

Drizzle with olive oil and sprinkle with sea salt and black pepper.

Repeat order a second time with remaining half of the ingredients.

Bake covered for 45 minutes. Remove cover and cook an additional 15 minutes until cheese is slightly golden brown.

Let sit for 10-15 minutes before serving.

kristen: *We became masters at making this recipe after watching our Grammy make this with love and perfection many times on our summer vacations Up North.*

sautéed spinach

Serves 4

Heat olive oil in large skillet. Add onions and sauté until tender and slightly browned.

Add chopped garlic to onions and heat for 1 minute, careful not to burn.

Add the baby spinach to the onions and garlic and toss to wilt. Continue adding spinach until the whole box has been added.

Once the spinach has wilted sufficiently, sprinkle in the sea salt and black pepper to taste, and grate in a few strokes of fresh nutmeg.

Place spinach in a serving dish and squeeze on lemon. Serve immediately.

2 tablespoons extra virgin olive oil

1 large onion, sliced into small wedges and separated

2 cloves garlic, chopped

1 11-ounce box organic baby spinach

Sea salt & black pepper

Fresh nutmeg

½ lemon

tip ▶ Almost any variety of greens like kale, collard greens, and Swiss chard can be made this way. Remove the thick stems from the leaves. Because kale leaves are a bit rougher than other greens, you may want to submerge and rinse in a large bowl of cold water; ring out and let dry.

 We all know that eating your greens provides many benefits, but did you know they are a good source of calcium? Leafy greens are also high in vitamin C helping to keep your immune system healthy and prevent sickness.

veggie stuffed peppers

Serves 6

Preheat oven to 375°F.

In a small pot, bring broth to a boil and add in rice. Once rice mixture begins to boil, cover and cook on a low simmer for 40-45 minutes.

Remove from heat and set aside to cool slightly.

Slice peppers in half and remove seeds and stems.

Place peppers cut side up on a lightly greased 9x13 inch baking dish.

In a large bowl combine rice and the remaining ingredients except cheese, and spoon mixture into peppers.

Cover baking dish with foil and cook for 30 minutes. Remove foil and top stuffed peppers with cheese.

Bake uncovered for an additional 15 minutes. Let cool for 5 minutes and serve.

1 cup organic brown rice

2 cups organic chicken broth

3 bell peppers

½ cup asparagus, chopped

½ cup Brussels sprouts, stems removed and sliced

½ cup mushrooms, chopped

½ cup broccoli florets

½ cup cauliflower florets

½ cup green onion, finely chopped

¼ cup basil, finely chopped

2 cloves garlic, minced

1 cup organic marinara sauce

½ cup feta or goat cheese, crumbled

fried rice

Serves 4

1½ cups organic brown basmati rice

2-3 eggs

½ cup diced carrots

½ cup diced onion

½ cup frozen peas

1 tablespoon extra virgin olive oil

1 tablespoon roasted sesame seeds

½ teaspoon black pepper

½ teaspoon sea salt

2 tablespoons Bragg's Liquid Aminos or low sodium soy sauce

1 teaspoon toasted sesame oil

Garnish with chopped green onions

Cook rice according to package directions. Rinse cooked rice in a strainer, and set aside to cool and dry slightly.

Scramble the eggs lightly in a small frying pan. They will continue to cook slightly when added into the rice. Set aside.

Heat the olive oil in a large frying pan over medium high heat. When the oil is very hot, add the onions and carrots. Stir constantly so that the vegetables don't burn.

When the onions and carrots are soft, add the peas and rice, and mix together. Cook for 5 minutes.

Chop the scrambled eggs and add them to the rice. Stir to combine.

Season with salt and black pepper. Sprinkle in the sesame seeds.

Add the sesame oil and Bragg's and cook for 3 more minutes.

tip ▶ Serve this dish hot with any Asian inspired entrée. To make a one-dish entrée, add diced, cooked chicken, beef, or shrimp.

farro & vegetables

Serves 4

1 cup farro, rinsed

3 cups organic vegetable broth

1 cup broccoli florets

1 cup cauliflower florets

1 cup of mushrooms, sliced

½ cup chopped red onion

½ bag organic frozen edamame, thawed

1 cup spinach or kale, chopped

Sea salt & black pepper

Bring farro and broth to a boil, and simmer for 30 minutes or until liquid is absorbed.

Heat 1 tablespoon extra virgin olive oil in a large skillet over medium-high heat. Add in broccoli, cauliflower, mushrooms, and red onion.

Cover and cook for 5 minutes.

Add in edamame and heat through.

Stir in spinach or kale and cook for 1-2 minutes or until slightly wilted.

In a large bowl, mix together the farro and vegetables. Season to taste with salt and black pepper and serve along with your favorite entrée.

tip ▶ Add your favorite fixings to farro or clean out leftover vegetables from the refrigerator for a delicious plant-based side dish.

 Farro is one of the oldest grains cultivated by humans and is a great source of both protein and fiber.

fiesta quinoa

Serves 4

Bring quinoa and broth to a boil, and simmer for 15 minutes or until liquid is absorbed.

Heat 1 tablespoon extra virgin olive oil in a large skillet over medium-high heat.

Add in peppers and onion, and cook until tender, about 5 minutes.

Add in beans and corn, and heat through, about 2-3 minutes.

In a large bowl combine quinoa and vegetables, and season to taste with salt and black pepper.

Serve in individual bowls and top with cheese, guacamole, and Greek yogurt.

1 cup quinoa, rinsed

2 cups organic vegetable broth

1 tablespoon extra virgin olive oil

1 orange bell pepper, chopped

1 yellow bell pepper, chopped

1 yellow onion, chopped

1 14-ounce can organic black beans, rinsed and drained

1 14-ounce can organic sweet corn, rinsed

2 tomatoes, chopped

½ cup organic cheddar cheese, shredded

1 cup guacamole (see Guaca-Money recipe page 56)

1 6-ounce container organic plain Greek yogurt

pearl couscous & figs

Serves 4

1 cups black mission figs, diced

1 cup tricolor pearled couscous

3 green onions, white and green parts, sliced thin

½ cup pistachios, chopped

¼ cup parsley, chopped

2 tablespoons extra virgin olive oil

2 tablespoons lemon juice

Sea salt & black pepper

Place diced figs in a bowl and add ¼ cup boiling water. Cover with plastic wrap and set aside to soften.

Cook couscous according to package directions. Put cooked couscous in a serving bowl.

Drain the water from the figs and add them to the couscous.

Add the green onions, pistachios, and parsley.

Add olive oil and lemon juice, and season with salt and black pepper to taste.

tip ▶ Can be served chilled.

desserts

meringue date cookies

Makes 24 cookies (pictured on page 174)

Preheat oven to 300°F.

Add salt to egg whites and beat to a stiff foam.

Sift together powdered sugar and flour. Add one tablespoon at a time to the egg whites, mixing thoroughly between each addition. Continue beating until very stiff. Fold in nuts, dates, and vanilla.

Drop from teaspoon onto cookie sheet lined with parchment paper.

Bake for 30 minutes.

3 egg whites, room temperature

¼ teaspoon sea salt

1¾ cups powdered sugar

1 teaspoon flour

1 cup pecans, broken

1 cup pitted dates, chopped

1 teaspoon vanilla extract

kristen:
These cookies are a Holiday favorite passed down from our Great Grandma Kramer. Grandpa "Gido" is the official taste tester with the same response every year. "Mmmmm... these are better than last year." We share this family recipe with you because we would hate for anyone to miss out on this delicious experience.

dark chocolate blueberry almond clusters

Makes 8

Preheat a double boiler over medium heat and add chocolate chips to melt.

Meanwhile, cover a baking sheet with wax paper.

Pile 8 small clusters of blueberries and almonds on baking sheet.

Pour melted chocolate over clusters and freeze for 5 minutes to harden.

Store in the refrigerator.

¼ cup fresh blueberries

¼ cup whole almonds

1 package dark chocolate chips

raw date cookies

Serves 10

Add almonds to a food processor and grind to a fine meal. Remove from processor and set aside.

Add walnuts to food processor and pulse until finely ground. Add dates to walnuts in food processor to combine. Add coconut and vanilla extract to walnut mixture until combined.

Form mixture into 1-inch balls and roll in almond meal.

tip▶ For tailgate season form date mixture into football shapes and roll in almond meal. Use white decorating gel to draw laces on football-shaped cookies

½ cup almonds

1 cup walnuts

1 10-ounce container pitted dates

½ cup shredded coconut

1 teaspoon vanilla extract

buckeye bark

Makes 15-20 pieces

Line a cookie sheet with waxed paper.

Melt 1 bag of chocolate chips in a double boiler. Spread the melted chocolate in a thin layer over waxed paper lined cookie sheet. Place in freezer for 10 minutes to harden.

Mix crunchy almond or peanut butter with agave nectar and vanilla extract.

Remove melted chocolate from freezer and spread nut butter mixture evenly over the top. Place in freezer for another 5 minutes to harden.

Melt the 2nd bag of chocolate chips and spread on top of frozen nut butter mixture. Return to freezer for 1 hour.

Once chocolate peanut butter mixture is hardened, break into medium-sized pieces and serve.

2 bags dark chocolate chips

1 jar crunchy almond or peanut butter

1 tablespoon agave nectar

1 tablespoon vanilla extract

tip▶ Choose nut butters that have one ingredient. Example: peanuts.

holly's oatmeal raisin cookies

Makes 12 Cookies

Preheat oven to 350°F.

Whisk together the eggs and vanilla. Add the raisins and cover for 1 hour, allowing raisins to become soft.

In medium bowl, sift together the flour, cinnamon, and baking soda.

Cream together the butter, virgin coconut oil, and sugars. Add flour mixture and combine (mix will seem dry). Mix in the egg and raisin mixture. Finally, add in oatmeal and combine.

Grease a cookie sheet with virgin coconut oil and drop the dough in ¼ cup balls 2 inches apart. Flatten each ball slightly using your palm.

Bake 10-12 minutes in the preheated oven, or until golden brown. Cool slightly, remove from sheet to wire rack. Cool completely.

2 eggs

1 teaspoon vanilla extract

1 cup raisins

1⅔ cup all-purpose flour

1 teaspoon cinnamon

2 teaspoons baking soda

⅓ cup unsalted butter (room temperature)

⅓ cup virgin coconut oil at room temperature (should not be liquid)

⅔ cup brown sugar

⅔ cup white sugar

1⅓ cup rolled oats

holly: *Matt is a fabulous cook and loves to create new recipes, but he doesn't like to bake because he'd rather experiment than follow precise directions. Luckily, baking is my passion, so we make a great team!*

no-bake cookies

Makes 12 cookies

Heat cocoa, sugar, milk, butter, and virgin coconut oil over medium heat. Heat these very, very slowly to a boil. Boil them for no longer than 90-120 seconds and remove from heat.

Mix together oats, peanut butter, and vanilla with a big wooden spoon or mixer.

Pour the hot mix over the oatmeal mix. Stir together for 4 minutes to allow oats to absorb liquid.

Using a large mixing spoon, drop spoonfuls on wax paper and let cool.

3 tablespoons unsweetened cocoa powder

2 cups cane sugar

½ cup skim milk

¼ cup butter

¼ cup virgin coconut oil

3 cups rolled oats

½ cup natural peanut butter

1 tablespoon vanilla extract

trail mix treats

Combine nuts, seeds, and dried fruit and set aside.

Melt 1 bag of dark chocolate chips over a double boiler.

Line a baking tray with waxed paper. Using a ladle, drop small dollops of melted chocolate on the waxed paper.

Sprinkle chocolate with trail mixture and let cool.

¼ cup pumpkin seeds

¼ cup whole almonds

¼ cup dried cranberries or cherries

¼ cup raisins

1 bag dark chocolate chips

tip ▶ For convenience, choose store-bought trail mix combinations that include raw nuts, and dried fruits without added oil or sugar.

banana bread

Serves 10-12

Preheat oven to 325°F.

Beat together the sugar and eggs on medium until light and fluffy, roughly 5 minutes.

Very slowly, drizzle in the oil, still beating the mixture on medium. Then add the applesauce and continue mixing.

Add the banana, Greek Yogurt, honey, and vanilla. Mix together on low speed until combined.

Combine the flour, baking soda, cinnamon, and sea salt, and fold into the banana mixture until thoroughly combined. Stir in the toasted walnuts.

Pour the batter into a greased 9x5 inch loaf pan.

Bake for 50-55 minutes, until toothpick comes out clean.

½ cup white sugar

2 eggs

¼ cup and 1 tablespoon virgin coconut oil (melted)

¼ cup applesauce

3½ ripe bananas, mashed with a fork to remove all lumps

2 tablespoons plain Greek yogurt

½ cup plus 2 teaspoons honey

1 teaspoon vanilla extract

1½ cups whole wheat flour

1 teaspoon baking soda

¼ teaspoon cinnamon

½ teaspoon sea salt

¾ cup walnuts, toasted

 This is a healthy spin on your traditional banana bread. It makes for a great gift from the kitchen.

chocolate chip peanut butter banana bread

Serves 10-12

1 cup white whole wheat flour

⅓ cup pure cane sugar

⅓ cup brown sugar, packed

1 teaspoon baking powder

½ teaspoon baking soda

¼ teaspoon sea salt

3 very ripe bananas, mashed

⅓ cup natural crunchy peanut butter

2 tablespoons plain nonfat Greek yogurt

1 large egg

1 teaspoon vanilla extract

2 tablespoons virgin coconut oil

¾ cup dark chocolate chips

Preheat oven to 350°F.

Combine flour, sugars, baking powder, baking soda, and sea salt into a small mixing bowl.

In a medium bowl mix together the bananas, peanut butter, Greek yogurt, egg, vanilla, and oil.

Fold in flour mixture until thoroughly combined and then gently fold in chocolate chips.

Pour the batter into a greased 9x5 inch loaf pan.

Bake for 30-45 minutes, or until toothpick comes out clean.

Cool in pan for 15 minutes. Carefully remove from pan and allow to cool completely on wire rack before slicing.

dessert dip

Serves 4-6

Combine first 4 ingredients in a food processor and blend until smooth.

May use immediately as a frosting or freeze for 15 minutes to serve as a mousse/dip.

Serve with your favorite dippers.

½ cup natural creamy peanut butter

¼ cup virgin coconut oil

½ can original coconut milk (use only the hardened cream that forms on the top of the can)

1 tablespoon light agave nectar

Toppings:
Dark chocolate chips

Cacao nibs

Toasted coconut

Fresh berries

Dippers:
Banana slices

Apple slices

Cookies

tip▶ Look for BPA-free canned coconut milk. Canned coconut milk is a mixture of coconut water and coconut cream. It is natural for the water and cream to separate as the can sits.

whipped coconut cream

Serves 2

1 can original coconut milk

1 teaspoon vanilla extract

Place can of coconut milk in refrigerator for 2 hours so the cream separates from the coconut water.

Open the can and scoop out just the hardened cream that forms on the top and add to a mixing bowl.

Save the remainder of the coconut water to use at another time.

Add vanilla extract to coconut cream and mix with a handheld mixer until it achieves a whipped cream consistency.

tip ▶ The hardened cream that forms on the top of canned coconut milk makes for a delicious fluffy dessert topper.

coconut butter frosting

Makes 2 cups of frosting

Combine virgin coconut oil, coconut manna, 1 cup of powdered sugar, and vanilla extract in a large bowl. Blend with a handheld mixer until well combined.

While beater is running, add powdered sugar and milk alternately, ¼ cup at time until remainder of powdered sugar is used and frosting is desired consistency. Use more milk for a thinner frosting or icing consistency.

Use immediately or place frosting in refrigerator in an airtight container.

If using refrigerated frosting, let soften at room temperature for 1 hour before using. Frosting will last in the refrigerator for 4-5 days.

½ cup virgin coconut oil, softened

¼ cup coconut manna (coconut butter), softened

1 16-ounce package organic powdered sugar

1 tablespoon vanilla extract

½ to 1 cup original almond milk

tip▶ Coconut Manna is made when dried coconut meat is ground into a very fine pulp resulting in a butter consistency.

Coconut manna is solid at room temperature and usually separates into two layers. The upper translucent layer is the virgin coconut oil and the lower opaque layer is the coconut meat.

To use, warm the jar up in a pot of hot water and stir to combine.

Coconut manna tends to have a richer flavor than virgin coconut oil and can be used in place of butter or nut butters.

banana ice cream

Serves 2

3 frozen bananas (peel and freeze overripe bananas for future use)

2 tablespoons cashew butter (can use any nut butter)

2 tablespoons dark cacao nibs

Cut frozen bananas into 1-inch slices.

Place in food processor and blend until creamy, about 30 seconds.

Add in cashew butter and blend to mix. Top with dark cacao nibs and enjoy!

Feel free to enjoy banana ice cream plain or add your own favorite toppings!

 Skip the ice cream and go for a banana ice cream instead! As the food processor blends the frozen bananas, it generates heat which causes the bananas to turn into a frozen yogurt consistency. Add your favorite toppings and enjoy a healthy sundae loaded with potassium, fiber, and antioxidants.

sherbet delight

Serves 4

10 ounces frozen strawberries

2 large bananas

4 dates (pitted)

½ cup raw almonds (soaked in water for 2 hours)

½ cup almond milk

Shredded coconut and cacao nibs for garnish

Combine all ingredients in a food processor and blend until smooth. Top with coconut and cacao nibs.

 Cacao nibs are a healthy magnesium-rich substitute for chocolate chips.

apple crisp

Serves 8

5 pounds apples, peeled and sliced

2 teaspoons cinnamon

2 cups rolled oats

1 cup whole wheat flour

¼ cup packed brown sugar

¼ teaspoon sea salt

1 teaspoon baking powder

2 eggs

½ cup organic virgin coconut oil, melted

Preheat oven to 325°F.

Toss apples with cinnamon and arrange in bottom of a 9x13 inch pan.

Mix dry ingredients together in a medium bowl.

Lightly beat eggs and add to dry ingredients. Gently work in eggs until mixture is crumbly.

Spread mixture on top of apples.

Pour melted virgin coconut oil evenly over the top of the mixture.

Bake 1 hour.

 Cinnamon is considered a super spice and is especially beneficial for balancing blood sugar and keeping energy level steady.

raw banana
pecan pie

Serves 8

To make the crust:

Grind the first 3 ingredients in a food processor until finely ground. Press mixture evenly into an 8-inch pie dish.

To make the filling:

Blend dates, overripe bananas, and lemon juice in the food processor until smooth.

Fold in banana slices and pour combined mixture into the pie crust.

Sprinkle about 1 tablespoon of chopped pecans on top, cover with plastic wrap, and refrigerate for a couple hours.

For the crust:

1 cup raw pecans

1 cup dates, pitted

½ teaspoon vanilla extract

For the filling:

5 dates, pitted

3 overripe bananas

1 tablespoon fresh lemon juice

1 banana, sliced

1 tablespoon pecans, chopped

tip ▶ To make raw pie crusts, simply use a 1:1 ratio of dried fruit to nuts.

spirulina birthday pie

Serves 8

For the crust:

2 cups raw almonds, finely ground in food processor

⅓ cup dried figs, chopped (2-3 figs)

1 tablespoon agave nectar or raw honey

For the filling:

¾ cup coconut water

¼ cup raw cashews

¼ cup virgin coconut oil

1 tablespoon agave nectar or raw honey

1 tablespoon crushed spirulina and chlorella tablets

Toppings:

1 tablespoon cacao nibs

Nuts of choice

To make the crust:

Combine ground almonds and figs in a food processor and pulse until fine crumbles.

Transfer almond fig mixture to a mixing bowl.

Add agave nectar and mix well to form a crust like consistency. Press the crust mixture evenly into the bottom and sides of an 8-inch pie tin.

For the filling:

Combine all of the filling ingredients in a high-speed blender or food processor and blend until smooth.

Pour the mixture into the pie crust and top with cacao nibs and your favorite nuts.

Freeze for at least one hour or overnight.

Remove from freezer 20 minutes before serving.

kristen: *No one should go without spirulina pie on their birthday! I make this for my dad every year. It is a true superfood dessert.*

fruitilicious upside-down cake

Serves 4

Combine the pecans, dates, and vanilla in a food processor and pulse until finely ground.

Line a small mixing bowl with saran wrap. The bowl should be approximately 7 inches wide, by 3½ inches deep to allow ingredient layers to be seen when served.

Layer kiwi slices in rows along bottom and up the sides of bowl.

Press half of the pecan and date mixture evenly over the kiwi slices to secure in place. Push date mixture in the spaces between the kiwi slices.

Layer banana slices, blueberries and raspberries over the pressed pecans and dates.

Cover the fruit layers with the second half of the pecan and date mixture, and press to seal.

Push down so the top is level with the edges.

Wrap in saran wrap and place in refrigerator for 20 minutes to set.

To serve, remove top layer of saran and place serving dish on bowl. Flip the bowl and plate, and remove the bowl from the filling. Remove saran wrap.

Cut into slices and serve.

2 cups raw pecans

2 cups pitted dates

1 teaspoon vanilla extract

2-3 kiwis, peeled and sliced

2-3 bananas, sliced

1 pint blueberries

1 pint raspberries

 Nothing is sweeter than nature's candy – fresh fruit.

index

d

e

h

i

j

k

l

GET HEALTHIER INSIDE AND OUT!

We all want to bring our best and healthiest selves to life at home, at work, and at play. The ingredients are simple: get enough rest, eat healthy foods, and move your body daily—REST EAT MOVE. These simple principles are the foundation of On Target Living!

Simple? In theory! But knowing what to do and how to do it can be extremely challenging. A poor food environment, lack of movement, over medication, and the demanding pace of daily life continually contribute to a downward spiral of health for many.

On Target Living offers focused strategies to help people reach optimal health, balance, energy, and vitality through:

- Prioritizing rest and rejuvenation
- Developing healthy eating habits
- Incorporating exercise into daily routines

On Target Living provides the tools necessary to improve:

- Cholesterol Balance
- Sustainable Weight Loss
- Type 2 Diabetes
- Blood Pressure
- Acid Reflux
- Hormonal Health
- Sleep
- Energy

On Target Living works with organizations to achieve greater health and performance through:

- Keynotes/Seminars
- Executive Team Training
- Retreats
- Executive Private Experience
- On Line Coaching
- WebinarsTeleseminars
- Educational Resources
- Website/Newsletter

Find these products and more at:
ontargetliving.com/shop

OFFERING THE BEST
SO YOU FEEL YOUR BEST

On Target Living Essentials offers products we believe are "essential" to optimal health, performance, and well-being.

We have gathered together the best quality products on the market today to help you take "Small Steps to Healthy Living," the On Target Living lifestyle – REST EAT MOVE!

- Taking care of your body and your home/work environment
- Providing you with nutritious and delicious healthy eating options
- Facilitating your fitness activities at home

All are brands we have grown to know and trust. . . and use ourselves!

On our website, **ontargetliving.com/shop**, you will find:
- Nutrient-dense superfoods
- Favorite food upgrades
- Natural skin care products
- Eco-friendly, chemical-free cleaning products
- Fitness essentials such as tubing, foam rollers, and more

On Target Living Essentials make the On Target Living lifestyle nutritious, delicious, manageable and affordable.

Learn more about On Target Living and a complete list of services, products, and resources on our website: **ontargetliving.com.**

ontargetliving.com   #targettotable